RETHINKING GOD'S WILL

LEARNING TO LIVE CONFIDENTLY IN CHRIST

ROBERT GRIFFITH

GRACE AND TRUTH PUBLISHING
P.O. Box 338, Gunnedah NSW 2380 Australia
www.graceandtruthpublishing.com.au

ISBN: 978-1-7642635-8-0

For all who desire to follow God faithfully, and need to be reminded that His will is not a destination to reach, but a relationship to live within.

TABLE OF CONTENTS

PREFACE

There's not an issue which troubles Christians more persistently than the question of God's will. It surfaces in our moments of decision and crisis, in seasons of transition and uncertainty, and often in quiet, anxious reflection. *Am I in God's will? What if I make the wrong choice? How can I know what God wants me to do next?*

For many believers, the search for God's will often becomes an exhausting pursuit. Instead of producing confidence, it breeds fear. Instead of deepening trust, it encourages hesitation. Instead of anchoring faith in Christ, it subtly shifts attention inward, bringing constant self-examination and the pressure to 'get it right.' This book was written because I believe that much of that anxiety is completely unnecessary and totally unbiblical.

Over my many years in pastoral ministry, I have encountered countless sincere Christians who love God deeply and yet they live with a lingering sense of uncertainty about their lives. They pray earnestly, search for signs, seek confirmation, and worry about missing God's plan. Often, this happens not because they take the Bible lightly, but because they take it seriously and want to honour God in every decision they make. Yet within that seriousness, something vital is too often overlooked.

The New Testament presents a radically different starting point for understanding God's will. It does not begin with decisions, directions, or divine blueprints. It begins with Christ. God's will, at its heart, is not primarily about *what* we do, but about *who* we are becoming.

The Bible states this quite plainly: *"For those God foreknew he also predestined to be conformed to the image of his Son."* (Romans 8:29). That purpose is not selective or hidden. It is the same for every single believer, and this conviction reshapes everything.

Therefore, if God's will is fundamentally about being formed into the likeness of Christ, then the Christian life is not a fragile tightrope walk where one wrong step will send us tumbling outside God's purposes.

The Christian life is a secure relationship in which our God is faithfully at work, shaping His people daily through the Bible, community, obedience, suffering, joy, wisdom, and grace. Our decisions still matter, but they are not the foundation of God's will. Christ is.

This book was also written because the Bible itself is so often mishandled in this area. I see this all the time. Verses about God's guidance, sovereignty, and purpose are frequently lifted out of context and placed alongside one another in ways that seem contradictory. On the one hand, the Bible strongly affirms God's purposeful will and sovereign care. On the other hand, it speaks clearly about freedom, responsibility, and wisdom. When these truths are not held together carefully, confusion always follows.

The Bible does not teach that believers must discover a hidden plan for their lives. Nor does it teach that God is indifferent to how His people live. Instead, it presents a life of faith marked by trust, obedience, wisdom, and freedom in Christ. *"It is for freedom that Christ has set us free."* (Galatians 5:1). That freedom is not a threat to faithfulness. It is the context in which it flourishes.

Throughout this book, I have tried to resist offering formulas, shortcuts, or simplistic answers. The Christian life is not lived by technique, but by relationship. God does not promise clarity at every turn. He promises His presence. *"Never will I leave you; never will I forsake you."* (Hebrews 13:5). That promise is more sustaining than certainty is.

This book is therefore not a guide to decision-making. It is an invitation to completely rethink how we understand God's will. It is an invitation to move away from fear-driven discernment and toward confidence rooted in Christ. It is an invitation to rest.

Rest does not mean passivity. It means trusting God with what He has never asked us to control. It means taking responsibility seriously without carrying anxiety unnecessarily. It means living faithfully in the ordinary rhythms of life, confident that God is at work even when the path ahead is unclear. *"The Lord will fulfil his purpose for me; your love, Lord, endures forever."* (Psalm 138:8).

If this book is to achieve its purpose, it will not eliminate every question you might have about God's will. But I hope and pray it will quieten the anxiety that all too often accompanies those questions.

I also hope it will strengthen your confidence in Christ, deepen your trust in the Bible, and free you to live faithfully without fear of missing God's purposes.

This is a timely reminder that God's will is not a puzzle to solve. It is the gracious, steady work of a faithful God forming His people in Christ.

My prayer is that as you read, you will discover that you are not standing on the edge of God's will, hoping not to fall. You are already standing within it, held securely by the One who is faithful in every season.

Robert Griffith

1. WHY GOD'S WILL FEELS SO CONFUSING

For many Christians, few questions generate as much confusion, anxiety, and hesitation as the question of God's will. Believers genuinely want to honour God with their lives. They want to live faithfully, obediently, and wisely. Yet when it comes to decisions about work, relationships, location, ministry, or the future more generally, the search for God's will all too often feel far more complicated than the Bible seems to suggest it should be.

This common confusion is not usually born out of rebellion or indifference. It arises precisely because believers care deeply about pleasing God. The problem is not a lack of sincerity, but a lack of clarity about what the Bible actually means when it speaks of God's will.

The Bible speaks frequently and confidently about God's will, yet so many Christians experience it as elusive and difficult to grasp. This disconnect raises an important question. If God's will is so central to faithful Christian living, why does it so often feel so unclear?

The fear of getting it wrong

At the heart of this confusion lies fear. Many believers approach the question of God's will with the underlying concern that there is a single correct path for their lives, and that missing it will have lasting consequences. This fear quietly shapes how they read the Bible, pray, and make decisions.

Yet the Bible consistently presents God as sovereign, purposeful, and secure in the outworking of His plans. God is not portrayed as anxious or reactive, nor as dependent on human precision for His purposes to succeed.

The psalmist makes it very clear, *"The Lord does whatever pleases him, in the heavens and on the earth, in the seas and all their depths."* (Psalm 135:6). God's will is never fragile. It is effective and unthreatened.

Similarly, the Bible reassures believers that God is actively at work in their lives, not merely observing from a distance. Paul writes in Romans 8:28, *"And we know that in all things God works for the good of those who love him, who have been called according to his purpose."*

God's purpose does not hang in the balance while believers try to discern the right choice. He is already at work, weaving even uncertainty and weakness into His good and sovereign design.

Yet despite these assurances, many Christians live as though God's will is narrow and easily missed. They assume that one wrong decision could permanently place them outside God's purposes. This assumption does not come from the Bible. It comes from a particular way of thinking about God's will that the Bible itself never teaches.

When God's will is treated like a hidden blueprint

Much confusion arises when God's will is imagined as a detailed blueprint for each individual life, known fully only to God and waiting to be discovered by us. In this framework, every decision carries enormous weight. Believers feel compelled to find the one correct option among many, fearing that choosing wrongly will derail God's plan for them.

But the Bible does not speak of God's will in these terms. It never encourages believers to uncover God's secret plans before acting. In fact, it explicitly draws a distinction between what God has revealed and what He has not.

"The secret things belong to the Lord our God, but the things revealed belong to us and to our children forever, that we may follow all the words of this law." (Deuteronomy 29:29). This verse is often overlooked, yet it provides crucial clarity. God has not promised to reveal every detail of His purposes. What He has revealed is sufficient for faithful living. Confusion sets in when believers attempt to live by what God has not revealed rather than by what He has made clear already.

When God's will is treated as hidden information that must be discovered before any action is taken, decision-making becomes paralysed. Prayer turns into an attempt to extract answers rather than a deep expression of trust. Faith becomes cautious and defensive rather than confident and active.

Confusing God's sovereignty with personal direction

Another source of confusion is the failure to distinguish between God's sovereign will and His guidance for daily life. The Bible speaks powerfully of God's sovereign purposes. In Isaiah 46:10 God declares, *"My purpose will stand, and I will do all that I please."* Nothing in heaven or on earth can thwart what God has determined to accomplish.

These statements are meant to reassure God's people, not burden them. They affirm that history is not random and that God's redemptive purposes will succeed. But when verses about God's sovereignty are applied directly to personal decision-making, they are misused.

God's sovereign will describes what God has already decreed will happen. It is not something believers are called to discover in advance. The Bible never instructs believers to seek out God's sovereign purposes for their individual lives before making decisions. Instead, as believers are called to simply trust that those purposes are secure.

When sovereignty is confused with guidance, anxiety grows. Believers begin to feel responsible for aligning themselves with God's decrees, as though God's plans depend on their discernment. The Bible presents the opposite picture. God's sovereignty is the reason believers can act without fear, not the reason they must hesitate.

The weight of decisions the Bible never places on us

Many Christians live under a weight that the Bible never places on them. Decisions about employment, marriage, relocation, or ministry are treated as moments of spiritual danger rather than opportunities for faithful living.

Believers may delay action indefinitely, waiting for clarity that the Bible has not promised. Yet the Bible consistently addresses believers as people who are capable of making real decisions. They are urged to grow in wisdom, to seek counsel, and to act thoughtfully. *"The simple believe anything, but the prudent give thought to their steps."* (Proverbs 14:15). Wisdom is not presented as an alternative to faith, but as an expression of it.

The New Testament assumes this posture as well. Believers are exhorted to discern what pleases God. *"Therefore do not be foolish, but understand what the Lord's will is."* (Ephesians 5:17). In context, this understanding is not about discovering hidden instructions, but about living wisely and faithfully in light of the gospel.

When Christians load decisions with expectations the Bible does not support, confusion is inevitable. The problem is not that God's will is unclear. The problem is that it is being asked to do something it was never meant to do.

When obedience is replaced by anxiety

Perhaps the most damaging effect of misunderstanding God's will is the way obedience is replaced by anxiety. Instead of focusing on what God has clearly commanded, believers become preoccupied with what God might want them to do next. Clear calls to love, holiness, generosity, and faithfulness are sidelined while believers instead search for guidance about their personal circumstances.

Yet the Bible consistently prioritises obedience to what God has already revealed. In 1 Thessalonians 4:3, Paul writes, *"It is God's will that you should be sanctified."* This is one of the rare places where the Bible explicitly states, "This is God's will," and it does so not in relation to personal direction, but in relation to holiness. Similarly, *"Give thanks in all circumstances; for this is God's will for you in Christ Jesus."* (1 Thessalonians 5:18). Again, God's will is presented as a way of living rather than a path to be discovered. These statements are clear, accessible, and demanding. They do not depend on special insight or personal revelation.

When believers neglect these clear expressions of God's will in favour of speculative guidance, anxiety takes over. The Christian life becomes an endless effort to avoid error rather than a confident pursuit of faithfulness.

A confusion the Bible intends to resolve

The confusion surrounding God's will is not inevitable. The Bible provides the clarity believers need, but that clarity comes from understanding what God's will actually refers to and how it functions in the Christian life. God's will is not primarily about managing individual outcomes. It is about forming a people who live faithfully before Him.

When God's will is understood in this light, fear begins to lose its hold. Believers are freed from the pressure to discover hidden plans. They are invited to trust God's sovereignty, obey His revealed will, and grow in wisdom as they live their lives before Him.

This shift does not make life simpler, but it makes it steadier. It replaces anxiety with confidence and paralysis with purposeful action. God's will no longer looms as an unsolvable puzzle. It becomes the secure framework within which believers can live, choose, and grow. That is where clarity begins.

One of the reasons confusion about God's will persists is that many believers approach the subject with expectations the Bible never creates. They assume that if God truly cares about their lives, He must provide specific direction for every significant decision. When that direction does not come in the way they expect, uncertainty is interpreted as failure, either on their part or on God's.

Yet the Bible consistently presents a different picture. God's concern is not primarily to direct every step in advance, but to shape the people who walk. the Bible does not portray faithful living as being dependent on constant guidance, but on trust, obedience, and growing wisdom.

When certainty is mistaken for faith

In many Christian circles, certainty has been elevated as a spiritual ideal. Being confident about God's will is seen as a mark of maturity, while uncertainty is treated as a spiritual deficiency. This deceptive mindset quietly reshapes the way believers think about faith. But the Bible never defines faith as certainty about the future. Faith is trust in God's character in the present. The writer of Hebrews describes faith not as knowing outcomes, but as *"confidence in what we hope for and assurance about what we do not see."* (Hebrews 11:1). Faith lives with unresolved questions. It does not require exhaustive information.

Abraham is repeatedly held up as an example of faith, yet his obedience often involved acting without clarity. *"By faith Abraham, when called to go to a place he would later receive as his inheritance, obeyed and went, even though he did not know where he was going."* (Hebrews 11:8). The Bible does not present Abraham as reckless or uninformed, but as trusting. His faith was expressed not in certainty, but in obedience which is grounded in confidence in God.

When believers equate faith with certainty, they inadvertently create a problem which the Bible does not recognise. They wait for assurance before acting, even when God has not promised to provide it. As a result, faith is then redefined as hesitation rather than trust.

The search for signs and impressions

Another common source of confusion is the expectation that God will communicate His will primarily through signs, impressions, or internal promptings. While the Bible affirms that God can guide His people in personal ways, it does not present this as the normal or necessary means by which God's will is known.

In fact, the Bible warns against seeking signs as a substitute for trust. Jesus rebukes those who demand signs before they will believe, saying, *"A wicked and adulterous generation asks for a sign."* (Matthew 16:4). The issue is not that God cannot give signs, but that reliance on them reveals a deeper problem of trust.

The Old Testament repeatedly shows that signs do not guarantee obedience or faithfulness. Israel witnessed extraordinary acts of God and still struggled with unbelief. The problem was not lack of information, but lack of trust. External confirmation cannot replace internal faithfulness.

When believers come to rely on impressions or signs to make decisions, anxiety often increases. Impressions are subjective. Signs are ambiguous, and the absence of confirmation can be paralysing. The Bible does not encourage believers to build their lives on such foundations. Instead, it calls them to live by faith informed by God's revealed Word.

In Psalm 119:105 we read, *"Your word is a lamp for my feet, a light on my path."* Notice that God's Word is described as light for the path, not a floodlight illuminating the entire journey. The Bible provides enough clarity for faithful steps, not exhaustive detail for every turn.

When God's will is reduced to personal fulfilment

Confusion about God's will is also fuelled by the very subtle assumption that God's primary concern is personal fulfilment. Many Christians assume that God's will for their lives must align with their deepest desires for happiness, success, or satisfaction. When circumstances are difficult or disappointing, they may conclude that something has gone wrong.

Yet the Bible consistently challenges this assumption. Jesus calls His followers to a path that includes sacrifice and loss. *"Whoever wants to be my disciple must deny themselves and take up their cross daily and follow me."* (Luke 9:23). God's will is not presented as a guarantee of ease, but as a call to faithfulness.

The apostle Peter echoes this in 1 Peter 3:17, *"For it is better, if it is God's will, to suffer for doing good than for doing evil."* This verse alone dismantles the idea that God's will is always synonymous with comfort or fulfilment. God's will may involve hardship, not because He is indifferent, but because He is committed to deeper purposes.

When believers assume that God's will must always feel good or lead to visible success, confusion is inevitable. Difficulty is interpreted as deviation. Suffering is seen as failure. The Bible presents a far richer and more demanding vision. God's will is oriented toward faithfulness, not fulfilment.

The misuse of guidance language

Much of the language Christians use about God's will sounds biblical yet carries assumptions the Bible does not support. Phrases like "God told me" or "God led me" are often used to describe personal decisions. While such language may reflect sincere conviction, it can also reinforce the idea that God's will operates primarily through private revelation.

The Bible uses guidance language carefully. When God speaks directly, the text usually makes it unmistakably clear. Prophetic revelation is not subtle or ambiguous. It is authoritative and public. The everyday life of faith, however, is not portrayed as a constant stream of divine instructions. Instead, believers are urged to seek wisdom. *"If any of you lacks wisdom, you should ask God, who gives generously to all without finding fault."* (James 1:5). Wisdom is not the same as revelation. It involves discernment, reflection, and growth. It requires engagement with reality rather than withdrawal from it.

The book of Proverbs repeatedly contrasts wisdom with folly, not guidance with misguidance. The assumption is that God's people will make choices, and that those choices can be wise or foolish. God's will is never discovered by avoiding decision-making, but by growing in wisdom.

Why confusion persists

When these misunderstandings combine, confusion becomes almost inevitable. Believers are taught to seek certainty where the Bible calls for trust. They are encouraged to look for signs where the Bible calls for wisdom. They are promised fulfilment where the Bible promises faithfulness. The result is a spiritual environment in which God's will feels perpetually out of reach.

Yet the Bible itself offers a far more stable foundation. God's will is not hidden behind a maze of decisions. It is revealed in His character, His purposes, and His commands. It is lived out through obedience, trust, and growth rather than discovered through techniques.

When believers begin to let the Bible, rather than assumption, define what God's will is and how it operates, confusion starts to give way to clarity. The pressure to get it right is replaced by the call to live faithfully. Anxiety loosens its grip, and confidence begins to grow.

The confusion surrounding God's will is very real, but it is not inevitable. The Bible does not leave believers in the dark. It calls them to a different way of understanding God's will, one that is grounded in trust rather than fear, and in faithfulness rather than certainty.

Another layer of confusion emerges when Christians assume that clarity about God's will, should precede obedience. Many believers hesitate to act because they believe they must first be certain that a particular decision reflects God's will. Obedience is so often delayed until confidence is achieved. Yet the Bible consistently reverses this order. Obedience flows from trust, not from certainty.

The psalmist captures this posture when he prays, *"Show me your ways, Lord, teach me your paths. Guide me in your truth and teach me, for you are God my Saviour, and my hope is in you all day long."* (Psalm 25:4–5). Notice that guidance is sought within a relationship of trust and hope, not as a prerequisite for action. The posture is humble dependence, not anxious calculation.

When waiting becomes disobedience

There is a kind of waiting that honours God, and there is a kind that quietly resists Him. The Bible affirms patience, but it never commends paralysis. When believers refuse to act because they fear making the wrong choice, waiting can become a subtle form of disobedience.

Jesus addresses this tendency in the parable of the talents. The servant who refuses to act does so out of fear, not faith. His explanation is revealing: *"I was afraid and went out and hid your gold in the ground"* (Matthew 25:25). Fear often masquerades as caution, but it results in unfaithfulness. The problem is not lack of instruction, but lack of trust.

The Bible repeatedly calls God's people to act on what they already know. *"Anyone, then, who knows the good he ought to do and doesn't do it, sins."* (James 4:17). This verse is striking because it locates responsibility not in discovering new guidance, but in responding to existing knowledge. Obedience is not suspended until certainty arrives.

When believers think they have to wait for clarity before acting, they ignore the clear commands God has already given. Love, generosity, forgiveness, honesty, and faithfulness are never contingent on special guidance. They are simply expressions of obedience and are available in every circumstance.

Treating God's will as a test

Confusion also deepens when God's will is treated as a test to be passed rather than a relationship to be lived. Decisions are framed as examinations, with success measured by correctness rather than faithfulness. This mindset places believers under constant pressure and fosters a fear-based spirituality.

The Bible never presents God's will this way. God is not setting traps for His people or evaluating them on their ability to decipher His intentions. He is forming them through grace. Paul reminds believers, *"For it is God who works in you to will and to act in order to fulfil his good purpose."* (Philippians 2:13). God's work precedes and sustains human action.

This truth should radically alter how decisions are understood. Believers are not left to navigate God's will alone. God is actively at work within them, shaping both their desires and their actions. The Christian life is not a solo examination. It is a shared journey.

When God's will is treated as a test, failure becomes terrifying. When it is rightly understood as a relationship, failure becomes formative. The Bible does not deny the seriousness of obedience, but it consistently situates it within grace.

The pressure to hear God perfectly

Many Christians today feel an unspoken pressure to hear God perfectly. They assume that mature believers will receive clear, unmistakable guidance, and that uncertainty indicates spiritual weakness. This expectation fuels confusion and discouragement.

Yet the Bible does not support this assumption. Even faithful servants of God often acted with limited understanding. The Apostle Paul speaks quite openly about making plans while acknowledging uncertainty. *"Now I hope to spend some time with you, if the Lord permits."* (1 Corinthians 16:7). His confidence rests not in perfect knowledge, but always in submission to God's sovereignty.

James also echoes this when he warns against presumption. *"You ought to say, 'If it is the Lord's will, we will live and do this or that.'"* (James 4:15). This is not a call to hesitation, but to humility. Plans are made. Actions are taken. God's will is honoured not by avoiding decisions, but by holding them loosely before Him.

The Bible does not demand flawless discernment. It calls for humble dependence. The expectation that believers must hear God with precision before acting places a burden the Bible never imposes.

When clarity is promised where the Bible does not promise it

Confusion is often reinforced by promises the Bible does not make. Believers are sometimes told that if they pray hard enough, wait long enough, or listen carefully enough, God will make His will unmistakably clear. When this clarity does not come, frustration sets in. Yet the Bible never guarantees that every decision will be accompanied by clarity. What it does guarantee is God's presence and faithfulness.

"Trust in the Lord with all your heart and lean not on your own understanding; in all your ways submit to him, and he will make your paths straight." (Proverbs 3:5–6). This well-known promise is often misunderstood. It does not promise advance knowledge of every step. It promises God's faithful direction as believers trust and submit to Him.

The imagery is relational, not mechanical. God straightens paths not by eliminating uncertainty, but by guiding His people as they walk in trust. The emphasis is not on insight, but on dependence.

How the Bible actually brings clarity

The Bible brings clarity not by answering every question, but by redefining the question itself. God's will is not primarily about choosing correctly between options. It is about living faithfully before God. When this shift takes place, much of the confusion dissolves.

Believers are no longer consumed by the fear of missing God's will. They are more concerned with honouring Him in whatever circumstances they may face. Decisions are made with prayer, wisdom, and counsel, but without that crushing weight of needing to be perfect.

The Bible consistently invites believers into this freedom. *"Stand firm, then, and do not let yourselves be burdened again by a yoke of slavery."* (Galatians 5:1). Fear-driven decision-making is a form of slavery. Faith-filled obedience is freedom.

The root of the confusion exposed

At its core, the confusion surrounding God's will is not about guidance, but about trust. Believers struggle not because God is silent, but because they have been taught to expect a kind of guidance God hasn't promised to give. When those expectations are corrected, clarity begins to emerge. God's will is not hidden behind perfect decisions. It is clearly revealed in His character, His purposes, and His commands.

It is lived out through trust, obedience, and growing wisdom. The Bible does not call believers to master God's will, but to trust the God whose will is good, pleasing, and perfect.

When this foundation is laid, the question of God's will no longer dominates the Christian life as a source of anxiety. It becomes part of a larger journey of faithfulness, where believers walk forward with confidence, knowing that God is at work in them and through them as they live before Him.

2. THE RISE OF BLUEPRINT CHRISTIANITY

If confusion about God's will feels widespread today, it did not arise in a vacuum. It has been shaped by a particular way of thinking that has gradually overtaken modern Christianity. This way of thinking assumes that God has a detailed, personalised plan for every believer's life and that faithfulness consists in discovering and following that plan precisely.

Over time, this assumption has become so familiar that many Christians barely question it. Yet when measured against the Bible, it proves far less biblical than it first appears.

What blueprint Christianity assumes

At the heart of blueprint Christianity lies a powerful assumption: that God has mapped out a specific life plan for each believer in advance, covering everything from career and marriage to location and ministry, and that the primary task of the Christian is to uncover that plan. God's will is therefore imagined as a hidden blueprint, known fully to God and partially revealed to those who listen carefully enough.

This model appears to honour God's sovereignty. It will speak frequently of God's plans, His purposes, and His control. It also appears to take obedience seriously. Believers are encouraged to wait, to pray, and to seek guidance before acting. On the surface, this sounds deeply spiritual.

Yet the Bible never instructs believers to approach life this way. The Bible does not portray God's will as a secret document waiting to be discovered. Nor does it describe faithfulness as dependent on believers uncovering God's private intentions for individual lives. Instead, the Bible consistently directs believers to trust God's sovereignty, obey His revealed commands, and grow in wisdom as they live before Him.

The problem with blueprint Christianity is not that it speaks of God's will, but that it defines God's will in a way which the Bible does not.

How sovereignty gets misapplied

Blueprint thinking most often begins with true statements about God's sovereignty and then draws conclusions the Bible never draws. The Bible clearly affirms that God is sovereign over all things. *"The Lord has established his throne in heaven, and his kingdom rules over all."* (Psalm 103:19). Nothing happens outside God's ultimate authority.

However, the Bible never turns this truth into a method for personal guidance. God's sovereignty is always presented as a source of confidence, not as a code to be cracked. When believers confuse sovereignty with direction, they begin to feel responsible for aligning themselves perfectly with God's decrees. Instead of resting in God's rule, they fear mis-stepping within it.

Isaiah records God's declaration, *"My purpose will stand, and I will do all that I please."* (Isaiah 46:10). This is meant to reassure God's people that His redemptive purposes cannot fail. It is not meant to suggest that believers must discern those purposes in advance before making ordinary decisions. Blueprint Christianity turns a promise of assurance into a burden of responsibility.

When sovereignty is misapplied in this way, the focus subtly shifts from trusting God to managing risk. Faith then becomes cautious. Decisions are delayed. Believers hesitate, not because they lack desire to obey, but because they fear stepping outside a plan they believe exists but cannot clearly see.

The influence of modern individualism

Another force driving this blueprint Christianity myth is modern individualism. In so many cultures, personal fulfilment, self-expression, and individual destiny are deeply valued. These assumptions inevitably shape how Christians think about God's will. As a result, God's will is often framed in highly personal terms. Believers ask, "What is God's plan for my life?" rather than, "How is God calling me to live faithfully as part of His people?" The Bible, however, speaks far more often about God's purposes for His people collectively, not as individuals.

Paul writes in Ephesians 1:5, that God *"predestined us for adoption to sonship through Jesus Christ, in accordance with his pleasure and will."* The focus here is not on individual life paths, but on God's gracious purpose to create a redeemed people in Christ. Blueprint Christianity subtly shifts attention away from this corporate vision and back onto the individual.

When individual destiny becomes central, decision-making becomes intensely personal and emotionally charged. Choices about work, marriage, or where we live are no longer evaluated primarily in terms of wisdom and faithfulness, but in terms of whether they align perfectly with a supposed personal plan. This heightens anxiety, fuels confusion and never honours God.

How blueprint thinking shapes Christian behaviour

The practical effects of blueprint Christianity are really easy to recognise. Believers feel pressure to wait for clarity before acting. Prayer becomes an exercise in seeking confirmation rather than cultivating trust. The Bible is searched for hidden clues rather than clear instruction. So many opportunities are missed because certainty has not arrived.

Ironically, this mindset often sidelines the very things the Bible emphasises most strongly. The many clear commands about love, generosity, holiness, and service are overshadowed by speculation about future decisions. Jesus' simple call, *"Seek first his kingdom and his righteousness."* (Matthew 6:33), is replaced with anxious questions about personal outcomes.

Blueprint thinking can also foster spiritual comparison. Those who claim strong impressions or decisive guidance are viewed as more spiritual. Those who act with wisdom but without dramatic certainty may feel inferior. The Bible offers no support for this hierarchy. Faithfulness is never measured by the intensity of one's guidance experiences.

Blueprint Christianity feels convincing because it promises control in an uncertain world. If God has a specific plan and will reveal it, then the future feels manageable.

Within this imagined reality, risk is minimised. Responsibility is softened. Believers can reassure themselves that waiting is always the safer option. Yet the Bible does not promise control. It promises God's presence. Jesus does not tell His disciples that they will always know where they are going. He tells them whom they are following. Jesus said in Luke 9:23, *"Whoever wants to be my disciple must deny themselves and take up their cross daily and follow me."* Following is relational, not informational.

The strong appeal of blueprint Christianity lies not in its biblical foundation, but in its emotional reassurance. It reduces the discomfort of uncertainty. But in doing so, it subtly undermines trust. Instead of learning to rely on God's faithfulness, believers learn to rely on perceived clarity.

A model the Bible never teaches

Perhaps the most telling indictment of blueprint Christianity is this: the Bible never teaches it. No passage instructs believers to uncover God's detailed plan for their lives. No biblical figure is commended for waiting until every decision was clarified in advance. Instead, the Bible consistently presents faithful people acting in trust, often without knowing the outcome.

The clarity the Bible offers is not about personal blueprints, it is all about God's character and purposes. *"Trust in the Lord with all your heart and lean not on your own understanding."* (Proverbs 3:5). The Bible says that trust, not insight, is our foundation. God's will is not a puzzle to be solved, but a life to be lived in Christ, through Christ and for Christ.

Understanding how blueprint Christianity developed and why it feels so compelling is essential if confusion about God's will is to be addressed. Until this model is recognised and questioned, believers will continue to feel the weight of expectations the Bible never places upon them.

Clarity begins not by seeking better guidance techniques, but by letting the Bible define what God's will actually is and how it is meant to function in the Christian life.

Blueprint Christianity does not usually announce itself as a new or alternative theology. It often presents itself as simple biblical faithfulness. Its language is familiar, its instincts feel cautious and reverent, and its practices are widely affirmed in Christian culture. This is why it has spread so easily and so quietly. Yet when its underlying assumptions are examined in the light of the Bible, significant problems begin to emerge.

How selective Bible reading fuels blueprint thinking

One of the primary ways blueprint Christianity gains traction is through selective use of the Bible. Certain verses are repeatedly quoted, often without careful attention to context, while others are consistently overlooked. Passages that speak about God's plans or purposes are lifted out of their redemptive setting and applied directly to individual decision-making.

For example, believers frequently appeal to verses that affirm God's intentionality, assuming they refer to personalised life plans. Yet the Bible often speaks of God's plans in corporate, covenantal, and redemptive terms. For example, through the prophet Jeremiah, God reassures His exiled people, *"For I know the plans I have for you... plans to prosper you and not to harm you, plans to give you hope and a future."* (Jeremiah 29:11). This promise is given to a nation in exile, not to individuals seeking guidance about personal choices. It speaks of God's faithfulness to His covenant people, not of a private blueprint for each life.

When such verses are detached from their context, expectations are created that the Bible never intended to fulfil. Believers assume God will provide comparable clarity for every decision they face. When that clarity does not come, confusion and disappointment follow. At the same time, the many passages that clearly emphasise wisdom, responsibility, and ordinary faithfulness receive far less attention. The Bible's repeated calls to discernment are often overshadowed by the hope of direct guidance. Yet Proverbs insists, *"The plans of the diligent lead to profit as surely as haste leads to poverty."* (Proverbs 21:5). The emphasis is not on discovering hidden plans, but on diligent and thoughtful action.

When narrative is turned into the norm

Another way blueprint Christianity is reinforced is by treating biblical narratives as normative guidance patterns. Stories in which God speaks directly to individuals are assumed to describe how God ordinarily leads all believers, for all time.

The Bible does record moments of direct divine instruction. God speaks to Abraham, Moses, and the prophets in unmistakable ways. But these moments are extraordinary, not routine. They occur at critical points in redemptive history and are recorded precisely because they are unusual.

Hebrews reminds believers that God's way of speaking has changed in a decisive way. *"In the past God spoke to our ancestors through the prophets at many times and in various ways, but in these last days he has spoken to us by his Son."* (Hebrews 1:1–2). The focus shifts from repeated individual revelations to the definitive revelation of Christ.

Blueprint Christianity often overlooks this shift. It assumes that personal revelation should function today as it did in earlier periods of redemptive history. As a result, believers may expect God to speak to them in ways the Bible does not promise. When such experiences do not occur, they may conclude that they are missing something spiritually.

Whilst I affirm that God continues to speak to individuals in special ways, the Bible never teaches believers to model their everyday decision-making on exceptional moments of divine intervention. Instead, it consistently calls us to live wisely in light of God's final and sufficient revelation in Christ.

The subtle erosion of wisdom

As blueprint thinking takes hold, wisdom is gradually sidelined. Those day-to-day decisions are no longer approached primarily through reflection, counsel, and discernment. Instead, believers wait for direction that will relieve them of responsibility. Yet the Bible places remarkable weight on wisdom as a central feature of godly living.

Wisdom is not portrayed as a lesser alternative to guidance, but as a gift to be sought and cultivated. *"The fear of the Lord is the beginning of wisdom."* (Proverbs 9:10). Wisdom always flows from reverent trust in God, not from some special insight into future outcomes.

The New Testament continues this emphasis. Believers are urged to live thoughtfully, making the most of their opportunities. *"Be very careful, then, how you live – not as unwise but as wise, making the most of every opportunity."* (Ephesians 5:15-16). This clear exhortation assumes that believers are actively engaged in evaluating their circumstances and acting responsibly within them. Blueprint Christianity often unintentionally discourages this engagement. Believers may hesitate to plan, evaluate, or decide, fearing that doing so reflects a lack of dependence on God. Yet the Bible never opposes wisdom to faith. It presents wisdom as an expression of faith.

How responsibility becomes a threat

Another serious consequence of blueprint Christianity is that responsibility comes to feel dangerous. If God has a specific plan that must be discovered, then taking initiative becomes risky. Acting without certainty feels presumptuous. Believers may delay decisions indefinitely, hoping for confirmation that never comes.

The Bible does not treat responsibility in this way. It addresses believers as moral agents who are accountable for how they live. The parable of the talents illustrates this point. The servants are expected to act responsibly with what they have been given. The one who refuses to act out of fear is rebuked, not praised (Matthew 25:24-30).

Responsibility, in the Bible, is not the enemy of faith. It is one of its expressions. Believers are called to act thoughtfully, trusting God with the outcome. *"Commit to the Lord whatever you do, and he will establish your plans."* (Proverbs 16:3). This verse does not promise advance knowledge of God's plans. It promises God's faithfulness as believers act in trust.

When responsibility is avoided in the name of spirituality, growth is stunted. Believers remain dependent in ways the Bible does never teaches. Blueprint Christianity very often fosters this dependency by encouraging waiting where the Bible calls for wisdom.

The cost to spiritual confidence

Over time, blueprint Christianity erodes confidence. Believers become unsure of their ability to discern wisely. They doubt their own judgement, even when it is informed by the Bible and counsel. They may feel spiritually inferior if they do not experience clear impressions or decisive guidance.

The Bible offers a different vision of maturity. Mature believers are those who have learned to discern good from evil through practice. *"Solid food is for the mature, who by constant use have trained themselves to distinguish good from evil."* (Hebrews 5:14). Discernment grows through use, not through avoidance. This confidence is not self-reliance. It is confidence in God's work within His people. God is forming believers who choose to live faithfully in a very complex world, not children who must be constantly directed.

Why blueprint Christianity persists

Despite these clear weaknesses, blueprint Christianity persists because it feels safe. It reduces risk, delays responsibility, and promises certainty. It appeals to a desire for reassurance in an uncertain world. Yet the Bible does not promise safety through certainty. It promises faithfulness through trust.

Jesus does not call His followers to map out their future. He calls them to follow Him daily. *"Therefore do not worry about tomorrow, for tomorrow will worry about itself."* (Matthew 6:34). Worry about the future is replaced not with information, but with trust in God's care.

Blueprint Christianity substitutes a quest for certainty for the call to trust. It feels spiritual, but it subtly reshapes faith into fear management.

The Bible invites believers into something far deeper and more demanding: a life of trust, obedience, and growing wisdom before God.

Recognising how blueprint Christianity operates is an essential step toward clarity. Until its assumptions are exposed and questioned, the confusion about God's will continues to feel inevitable. But the Bible offers a better way, one grounded not in hidden plans, but in revealed truth and faithful living.

Even when its weaknesses are exposed, blueprint Christianity remains deeply persuasive. It does not survive because it is biblically robust, it persists because it meets the emotional and psychological needs many believers carry. To move beyond confusion about God's will, those underlying drivers must be named honestly and brought into the light of the Bible.

Why blueprint Christianity feels spiritually safe

One reason blueprint Christianity persists is that it offers a sense of spiritual safety. If God has a specific plan for every detail of life, then the responsibility for outcomes seems to shift away from the believer. The primary task becomes discernment rather than wisdom. As long as one is sincerely "seeking God's will," failure can be explained as a lack of clarity rather than a failure of judgement.

This can feel comforting, especially in seasons of uncertainty or fear. Waiting appears safer than acting. Indecision can be baptised as humility. But the Bible never equates faithfulness with inactivity. God repeatedly calls His people to act in trust, even when outcomes are uncertain.

When Joshua was appointed to lead Israel, God did not provide a detailed blueprint for every decision ahead. Instead, He gave a promise of His presence and called Joshua to courage and obedience. *"Be strong and very courageous. Be careful to obey all the law my servant Moses gave you... For the Lord your God will be with you wherever you go."* (Joshua 1:7–9). God's assurance here is relational, not instructional. Presence replaces precision.

Blueprint Christianity subtly replaces this biblical assurance with a demand for certainty. It offers the illusion of safety while quietly eroding trust.

The false comfort of spiritual explanation

Another reason blueprint Christianity endures is that it provides some simple explanations for complex experiences. Success is attributed to obedience to God's plan. Difficulty is attributed to missing it. Life becomes easier to interpret, even if those interpretations are not accurate.

Yet the Bible consistently resists this kind of simplistic cause-and-effect thinking. The book of Job stands as a sustained rebuke of the idea that life's outcomes can be neatly traced to personal decisions. Job's suffering is not explained by anyone's error, and his friends are rebuked precisely because they assume that suffering must indicate failure.

Jesus Himself rejects this whole framework when He addresses suffering. When asked about a tragic event, He refuses to assign blame or identify hidden causes. Instead, He redirects attention toward repentance and trust (Luke 13:1–5). The Bible does not invite believers to decode God's will through circumstances. It invites them to trust God within them.

Blueprint Christianity promises understanding, but it delivers oversimplification. It offers answers which the Bible refuses to give and, in doing so, it serves to increase confusion rather than resolve it.

When caution is mistaken for maturity

In many Christian contexts, caution is praised as maturity. Those who wait the longest, speak least confidently, and act most hesitantly are often assumed to be the most spiritual. Those who act decisively are viewed with suspicion, even when their decisions are thoughtful and faithful. The Bible does not support this equation. While it warns against haste and presumption, it also warns against fear-driven hesitation.

Proverbs observes, *"Whoever watches the wind will not plant; whoever looks at the clouds will not reap."* (Ecclesiastes 11:4). Excessive caution can be just as unfaithful as reckless action.

Blueprint Christianity tends to elevate caution because it appears humble. But humility in the Bible is not indecision. It is trustful obedience. Mature believers are not those who never act without certainty, but those who have learned to act wisely without it.

The New Testament consistently addresses believers as people who are capable of discernment. They are exhorted to always test, evaluate, and choose what is good. *"Test them all; hold on to what is good."* (1 Thessalonians 5:21). This instruction assumes engagement, not withdrawal.

The damage to Christian maturity

Over time, blueprint Christianity stunts spiritual growth. When believers are trained to wait for direction rather than grow in discernment, their ability to exercise God-given wisdom remains underdeveloped. They become fluent in spiritual language but hesitant in responsibility.

This has real consequences. Decisions are delayed unnecessarily. Opportunities for service are missed. Fear is mistaken for faith. Instead of learning from experience, believers remain trapped in cycles of indecision.

Perhaps most damaging of all is the way blueprint thinking subtly undermines confidence in grace. If the Christian life is framed as a series of correct and incorrect choices, then peace becomes fragile. Assurance depends on having chosen well. Anxiety becomes a constant companion.

The Bible presents a very different vision of maturity. Growth involves learning to discern, to act, and to trust God with outcomes. Failure is not treated as catastrophic, but as formative. God's faithfulness is never suspended or withdrawn when His people stumble. *"The Lord upholds all who fall and lifts up all who are bowed down."* (Psalm 145:14).

Recovering a Biblical understanding of God's will

Moving beyond blueprint Christianity does not mean we must abandon our dependence on God. It means recovering the categories the Bible itself provides. God is sovereign over all things. God has clearly revealed His moral will. And God has entrusted many decisions to the wisdom of His people. When these categories are confused, fear thrives. When they are clarified, freedom grows. Believers are no longer burdened with discovering what God has not promised to reveal. They are anchored in what God has already made clear.

The Bible never presents God as a distant planner guarding secret instructions. It always presents Him as a faithful Father who delights in the growth of His children. *"If any of you lacks wisdom, you should ask God, who gives generously to all without finding fault"* (James 1:5). Notice that wisdom, not revelation, is the promised gift here. Prayer becomes less about extracting information and more about expressing trust. Decision-making becomes an arena for growth rather than anxiety. Responsibility is embraced rather than feared.

A necessary reset

Before genuine clarity about God's will can ever emerge, many believers need a reset. They need to unlearn assumptions that have quietly shaped their thinking for many years. This is not a rejection of faith, but a deepening of it. It is a return to the Bible's own priorities.

God's will is not a maze to be navigated perfectly. It is a life to be lived faithfully. It is not discovered through hidden insight, but expressed through trust, obedience, and growing wisdom. Once blueprint Christianity is recognised for what it is, its hold begins to loosen. Believers are freed from the pressure to get everything right and invited into the far richer calling of living faithfully before God. From this point, the path toward clarity becomes clearer. It does not begin with better techniques for guidance, but with a better understanding of how the Bible itself speaks about God's will and how it is meant to function in the Christian life.

3. WHAT DO WE MEAN BY 'GOD'S WILL'?

Much of the confusion surrounding God's will can be traced to a simple but significant problem: the phrase "the will of God" is used in the Bible in more than one way. When these uses are blurred together, believers are left trying to apply verses in ways they were never meant to function. Clarity begins when the Bible is allowed to define its own terms.

The Bible does not speak of God's will as a single, flat concept. It presents God's will in different senses, each serving a distinct purpose. Failure to recognise these distinctions has led many Christians to expect guidance where the Bible intends assurance, and certainty where the Bible calls for trust.

God's sovereign will: what God has decreed

In its most fundamental sense, the Bible speaks of God's will as His sovereign decree. This is God's will in the sense of what He has determined will happen. It is comprehensive, unthwartable, and ultimately mysterious to human beings.

The Bible affirms this repeatedly and without qualification. *"Our God is in heaven; he does whatever pleases him."* (Psalm 115:3). God's will, in this sense, is not a proposal or a preference. It is effective. What God wills, He accomplishes.

Isaiah 46:10 records God's own declaration of this truth: *"I make known the end from the beginning, from ancient times, what is still to come. I say, 'My purpose will stand, and I will do all that I please.'"* God's sovereign will governs history itself. Nothing lies outside its scope. This aspect of God's will is never presented as something believers are meant to discover in advance. The Bible explicitly distinguishes between what God has revealed and what remains hidden. *"The secret things belong to the Lord our God, but the things revealed belong to us and to our children forever."* (Deuteronomy 29:29). God's sovereign will belongs in the category of "secret things." It is purposeful, powerful, and very real, but it is not accessible to human investigation.

When believers attempt to discern God's sovereign will before acting, confusion inevitably follows. The Bible never invites God's people to peer behind the curtain of divine decree. Instead, it calls them to trust that God's purposes are secure, even when they are unseen.

Why God's sovereign will is not a guidebook

A crucial mistake so many Christians make is turning God's sovereign will into a guidebook for personal decisions. They assume that if God has decreed all things, then faithful living must involve discovering those decrees ahead of time. The Bible never draws this conclusion.

In fact, the Bible consistently treats God's sovereignty as a source of comfort rather than instruction. Paul writes, *"For from him and through him and for him are all things. To him be the glory forever!"* (Romans 11:36). This doxology follows a reflection on the mystery of God's purposes, not an explanation of how to uncover them.

God's sovereign will reassures all believers that history is not random and that their lives are not adrift. It does not relieve them of responsibility, nor does it provide a clear script for decision-making. Attempting to live by God's secret will places a burden on believers the Bible never intends them to carry.

This is why the Bible never commands believers to "find" God's sovereign will. Instead, it commands them to trust it. *"Trust in the Lord with all your heart and lean not on your own understanding."* (Proverbs 3:5). Dependence replaces certainty. Trust replaces insight.

God's revealed will: What God has made known

In contrast to God's sovereign will stands His revealed will. This refers to what God has clearly made known through the Bible. Unlike His decrees, God's revealed will is accessible, understandable, and binding on all believers. The Bible frequently speaks of God's will in this sense.

"It is God's will that you should be sanctified." (1 Thessalonians 4:3). This is not hidden. It is plainly stated. God's will, in this passage, is not about a personal decision but about moral transformation. Similarly, Paul exhorts believers, *"Give thanks in all circumstances; for this is God's will for you in Christ Jesus."* (1 Thessalonians 5:18). Again, God's will is presented here not as information to be discovered, but as a way of life to be embraced.

These verses are striking because of their simplicity. They locate God's will in holiness, gratitude, obedience, and faithfulness. They do not require special insight or personal revelation. They are addressed to all believers equally.

When the Bible speaks clearly about God's will, it almost always does so in this moral sense. God's will describes the kind of life He desires His people to live. It is concerned with character rather than circumstance, with faithfulness rather than location.

How confusion enters the picture

Confusion arises when these two senses of God's will are collapsed into one. Believers take verses about God's sovereign purposes and assume they apply directly to personal guidance. At the same time, they overlook or minimise the verses that explicitly state what God's will is.

The result is a distorted picture. God's revealed will, which the Bible makes plain, is treated as secondary. God's secret will, which the Bible withholds, is treated as primary. This reversal creates anxiety. Believers search for information God has not promised to give, while neglecting obedience to what God has already revealed.

The Bible consistently points us in the opposite direction. God's people are called to obey what is clear and trust what is hidden. They are not expected to manage God's purposes, but to live faithfully within them. Paul captures this posture well in Romans 14:12, *"So then, each of us will give an account of ourselves to God."* Accountability is rooted in obedience to what God has revealed, not success in uncovering what He hasn't.

The foundation for clarity

Understanding these basic distinctions lays a foundation for clarity. God's sovereign will assures believers that their lives are held securely within His purposes. God's revealed will directs them toward faithful living. When these are kept distinct, confusion begins to give way to confidence.

Believers are freed from the pressure to discover God's hidden plans. They are anchored in the responsibility to obey God's clear commands. Trust replaces anxiety. Faithfulness replaces fear.

This biblical framework does not answer every question about the future, but it provides something far more valuable: a stable way of living before God. As the Bible itself teaches clearly, *"The unfolding of your words gives light; it gives understanding to the simple."* (Psalm 119:130). Light comes not from secret knowledge, but from God's revealed truth.

Once the Bible is allowed to speak on its own terms, the phrase "God's will" begins to regain its clarity. It no longer functions as a source of confusion, but as a guide for faithful, confident living before God.

Alongside God's sovereign will and His revealed moral will, the Bible also speaks of God's will in a relational and experiential sense. This third use is often the most misunderstood, and it is here that much confusion about guidance takes root. When this aspect of God's will is isolated from the others, it easily becomes distorted.

God's will as wisdom applied

The Bible frequently describes God's will not as a set of clear instructions to be uncovered, but as wisdom to be applied. This is especially clear in passages that call believers to discern what pleases God. Rather than offering detailed directives, the Bible assumes that believers are capable of thoughtful, prayerful judgement. Paul exhorts the church, *"Therefore do not be foolish, but understand what the Lord's will is."* (Ephesians 5:17).

In context, this command is not about discovering secret information. It is about living wisely in a fallen world. Paul immediately connects understanding God's will with being filled with the Spirit, worship, gratitude, and wise use of time. God's will is understood not through revelation of details, but through a Spirit-shaped life.

This emphasis on wisdom explains why the Bible always places such weight on maturity. Believers are not expected to remain perpetually dependent on external direction. They are expected to grow in discernment. *"Do not conform to the pattern of this world, but be transformed by the renewing of your mind. Then you will be able to test and approve what God's will is – his good, pleasing and perfect will."* (Romans 12:2). God's will is always discerned through transformed thinking, not through secret insight.

The renewed mind is central here. God does not bypass human reasoning. He redeems it. As minds become shaped by truth, believers become increasingly able to recognise what aligns with God's purposes. God's will is not revealed apart from this process, but through it.

Why the Bible emphasises discernment

Discernment is a skill that must be developed. The Bible treats it as something that grows through practice, not something that appears instantly. The writer to the Hebrews describes mature believers as those *"who by constant use have trained themselves to distinguish good from evil."* (Hebrews 5:14). Discernment comes through engagement with life, guided by God's Word.

This has significant implications. If discernment grows through use, then avoiding decisions in the name of spirituality actually hinders growth. Believers who refuse to act until certainty arrives deprive themselves of the very process the Bible uses to produce maturity. God's will, in this sense, is not something believers find once and for all. It is something they learn to recognise more clearly over time. This learning process requires responsibility. It involves weighing options, seeking counsel, and acting in faith.

The Bible repeatedly affirms the value of counsel in this process. *"Plans fail for lack of counsel, but with many advisers they succeed."* (Proverbs 20:18). Seeking advice is not a sign of weakness or lack of faith. It is an expression of humility and wisdom.

The Holy Spirit and ordinary decision-making

When believers speak of the Holy Spirit's guidance, they often imagine dramatic experiences or unmistakable promptings. The Bible presents a quieter, steadier picture. The Spirit's primary work is not to provide constant direction, but to shape character, renew the mind, and produce fruit.

The Apostle Paul describes the fruit of the Spirit as qualities of character: *"love, joy, peace, forbearance, kindness, goodness, faithfulness, gentleness and self-control."* (Galatians 5:22–23). These qualities profoundly affect how decisions are made. A person shaped by love, patience, and self-control will approach choices differently from one driven by fear or impulse.

The Spirit also works through the Bible to shape judgement. Jesus promises that the Spirit will guide His disciples into truth (John 16:13). This guidance is not primarily about revealing personal plans, but about deepening understanding of what God has already revealed. The Spirit illuminates truth so that believers can apply it wisely.

This explains why the Bible rarely connects the Spirit's work with specific life directions. Instead, it connects the Spirit's work with holiness, understanding, and obedience. God's will is lived out as believers walk by the Holy Spirit, not as they wait for instruction.

Why this is not moral relativism

Emphasising discernment and wisdom does not mean that God's will becomes subjective or negotiable. The Bible maintains clear moral boundaries. God has spoken plainly about what honours Him and what does not. Discernment operates within those boundaries, never outside them.

Paul addresses this balance when he writes, *"Everything is permissible for me," you say – but not everything is beneficial. "Everything is permissible for me" – but I will not be mastered by anything."* (1 Corinthians 6:12). Freedom exists, but it is not absolute. Decisions are evaluated by their impact, their fruit, and their alignment with God's purposes.

This clear framework allows for genuine freedom without abandoning obedience. Believers are not seeking permission to do whatever they want. They are learning to choose what is wise, loving, and faithful. God's will is honoured not through rigid conformity, but through thoughtful obedience.

Holding the three uses together

Confusion arises when one sense of God's will is elevated at the expense of the others. God's sovereign will assures believers that His purposes are secure. God's revealed will directs them toward holiness and obedience. God's will as wisdom calls them to discernment and maturity.

When these are held together, a coherent picture soon emerges. Believers are not responsible for managing God's purposes. They are responsible for obeying what God has revealed and living wisely within it. They are not paralysed by uncertainty, nor are they left without guidance. The Bible consistently calls believers towards this balanced posture. *"The Lord confides in those who fear him; he makes his covenant known to them."* (Psalm 25:14). God's covenant is revealed. His purposes are trusted. His wisdom is learned over time.

A clearer way forward

Understanding how the Bible uses the language of God's will reshapes the way believers approach their lives. The pressure to uncover hidden plans gives way to the call to live faithfully. Anxiety is replaced by responsibility. Confusion yields to clarity. God's will is not a single thread that must be followed perfectly. It is a framework within which believers live, grow, and learn. The Bible does not promise exhaustive knowledge. It promises sufficient guidance for faithful living.

As these distinctions become clear, the question of God's will begins to settle into its proper place. It no longer dominates the Christian life as a source of fear. It becomes part of a larger call to walk humbly, think wisely, and trust deeply in the God who has revealed Himself clearly and faithfully in His Word. Once these biblical distinctions are understood, a significant shift takes place in how believers relate to God's will. The question is no longer "How do I uncover God's plan?" but "How do I live faithfully within what God has revealed?" This shift does not lower the seriousness of obedience. It grounds it more securely.

Why God's will is rarely about choosing between options

One of the most freeing realisations for many Christians is that the Bible rarely presents God's will as a matter of choosing between morally neutral options. The Bible spends very little time instructing believers on which job to take, where to live, or which opportunities to pursue. Instead, it consistently addresses how believers are to live wherever they find themselves. This silence is not an oversight. It reflects the Bible's priorities. God is forming people, not managing their schedules. Paul's letters are filled with commands about character, relationships, and faithfulness, but remarkably silent about personal logistics. Believers are urged to live wisely, not to wait for instruction. *"Whatever you do, whether in word or deed, do it all in the name of the Lord Jesus."* (Colossians 3:17). This exhortation assumes that believers will be doing many things not specifically commanded in the Bible. The call is not to avoid action until guidance arrives, but to act in a way that honours Christ.

When believers treat God's will as primarily about choosing between options, they will overlook this larger call. Faithfulness becomes reduced to decision accuracy not Christlike living.

The freedom the Bible actually affirms

The Bible affirms a surprising degree of freedom in the Christian life. This freedom is not an afterthought. It flows directly from the gospel. Believers are no longer under law, but under grace. They are no longer slaves, but children.

Paul speaks explicitly about this freedom: *"You, my brothers and sisters, were called to be free."* (Galatians 5:13). This freedom is not freedom from responsibility, but freedom for faithful living. It enables believers to act without fear of condemnation, trusting that God's grace is sufficient.

This freedom includes freedom in decision-making. The Bible does not portray believers as needing God's permission for every choice. Instead, it calls them to use their freedom wisely.

Peter put it well when he wrote, *"Live as free people, but do not use your freedom as a cover-up for evil."* (1 Peter 2:16). Freedom is framed by obedience, not by control.

Blueprint Christianity struggles to make sense of this freedom. It treats freedom as dangerous, something that must be tightly regulated through guidance. But the Bible treats freedom as essential to maturity.

Why responsibility is a gift, not a threat

With freedom comes responsibility. The Bible does not shy away from this connection. Believers are repeatedly addressed as responsible agents who will give an account of their lives. This accountability is not meant to terrify, but to dignify.

Paul writes, *"So then, each of us will give an account of ourselves to God."* (Romans 14:12). This statement assumes that believers are making real decisions for which they are responsible. God does not shield His people from responsibility by providing constant direction. He entrusts them with the privilege of acting wisely.

Responsibility is a sign of maturity. Children require constant instruction. Adults are expected to exercise judgement. The New Testament consistently treats believers as those who are growing into maturity.

"Until we all reach unity in the faith and in the knowledge of the Son of God and become mature." (Ephesians 4:13). Maturity involves discernment, initiative, and wisdom.

When responsibility is avoided in the name of seeking God's will, growth is hindered. Believers remain dependent in ways the Bible does not intend. God's will is never threatened by responsible action. It is honoured through it.

How God's will and human decisions work together

A common fear among believers is that human decisions might interfere with God's will. The Bible presents the opposite view. God's will is not fragile. It is robust enough to incorporate human choices without being undermined by them.

Joseph's story illustrates this clearly. After years of suffering caused by human wrongdoing, Joseph tells his brothers, *"You intended to harm me, but God intended it for good to accomplish what is now being done."* (Genesis 50:20). God's purposes were not dependent on perfect human decisions. They were accomplished through and despite them.

This vitally important truth is meant to reassure believers, not encourage carelessness. God's sovereignty does not excuse unfaithfulness, but it does remove the fear that one wrong step will derail His purposes. Believers are free to act responsibly, trusting God to remain sovereign over outcomes. The Psalmist echoes this confidence when he writes, *"The Lord will accomplish what concerns me; your love, Lord, endures forever."* (Psalm 138:8). God's purposes are not suspended while believers navigate life. They are actively being fulfilled.

Living within God's will rather than chasing it

Once God's will is clearly understood biblically, the posture of the Christian life changes. Believers stop chasing God's will as though it were somewhere ahead of them. Instead, they begin to recognise that they are already living within it. This does not eliminate the need for prayer or reflection. It reshapes their purpose. Prayer becomes less about seeking information and more about seeking alignment. *"Teach me to do your will, for you are my God."* (Psalm 143:10). The focus is not on discovering plans, but on learning faithfulness.

The Bible consistently encourages this posture. Believers are called to walk in step with the Spirit, to live lives worthy of the gospel, and to grow in love and holiness. God's will is not found in a moment of revelation. It is lived out over a lifetime of faithful obedience.

The clarity the Bible provides

The Bible does not answer every question believers ask about the future. It does something better. It clarifies what matters most. Let me stress again, God's will is not hidden in the details of life. It is revealed in His character, His commands, and His purposes.

So, when believers align themselves with what God has clearly revealed, much of the anxiety surrounding God's will simply falls away. They are set free to live wisely, act responsibly, and trust deeply. The search for God's will gives way to the practice of faithfulness.

This clarity does not make the Christian life simple, but it does makes it stable. God's will is no longer a source of fear or confusion. It becomes the framework within which believers live confidently before God, trusting that He is at work in them and through them as they walk by faith.

4. FREEDOM, RESPONSIBILITY, AND THE MYTH OF THE PERFECT CHOICE

One of the most persistent sources of anxiety for Christians is the belief that there exists a single 'perfect' choice for every decision in life, and that faithfulness depends on finding it. This belief often operates quietly beneath the surface, shaping how we pray, think, and act. It gives rise to the fear that one wrong step could place a person permanently outside God's will. However, the Bible offers a very different vision of freedom, responsibility, and faithful living.

The myth of the one right choice

The idea that there is only one correct option for every decision is deeply embedded in popular Christian thinking. Believers may assume that God has predetermined which job they should take, which house they should buy, or which church they should attend, and that their task is to discern this choice accurately. When clarity does not come, anxiety increases. When a decision is made, doubt often follows because, *"How can I be sure?"*

The Bible never presents life this way. Nowhere does the Bible teach that every decision has one single divinely mandated outcome that must be discovered in advance. Instead, it presents believers as people who are trusted to act wisely within the boundaries God has set.

Paul's words in 1 Corinthians 10:23 are revealing: *"I have the right to do anything,"* you say – but not everything is beneficial. *"I have the right to do anything"* – but not everything is constructive." This verse assumes genuine freedom. Multiple options may be permissible, even if not all are equally wise. The question is not which option is 'God's secret choice,' but which option is most beneficial, constructive, and faithful.

The myth of the perfect choice turns decision-making into a spiritual minefield. The Bible turns it into an opportunity for wisdom.

Freedom rooted in grace, not fear

Christian freedom is not an add-on to the gospel. It flows directly from it. Because believers are justified by grace, they are freed from the fear of condemnation. This freedom fundamentally reshapes how decisions are made.

Paul declares, *"Therefore, there is now no condemnation for those who are in Christ Jesus."* (Romans 8:1). This is not merely a theological statement. It has very practical consequences. If there is no condemnation, then believers are not living under the constant threat of having one wrong decision held against them.

This freedom does not mean that choices are meaningless or consequences irrelevant. It means that the believer's standing before God is 100% secure. Decisions are made from a place of acceptance, not in order to secure it. Fear-driven discernment is replaced by faith-driven responsibility.

Paul captures this balance when he writes, *"You were called to be free. But do not use your freedom to indulge the flesh; rather, serve one another humbly in love."* (Galatians 5:13). Freedom is real, but it is shaped by love and obedience. It is not a licence for self-centred living, but an invitation to faithful engagement. When freedom is misunderstood, believers either abuse it or avoid it. The Bible calls believers to embrace freedom wisely.

Responsibility as a mark of maturity

Freedom and responsibility always travel together in the Bible. God does not free His people in order to keep them dependent. He frees them so that they may grow freely into maturity. Responsibility is not a punishment. It is a sign of trust.

The New Testament consistently addresses believers as adults, as people who are capable of judgement and discernment. Paul urges the church, *"I speak to sensible people; judge for yourselves what I say."* (1 Corinthians 10:15). This is a remarkable statement. The apostle expects believers to weigh his teaching thoughtfully. Faithfulness involves active engagement, not passive reception.

Responsibility also means that believers must own their decisions. The Bible never encourages them to blame God for outcomes. James warns against this tendency: *"When tempted, no one should say, 'God is tempting me.'"* (James 1:13). God is never the author of moral failure, nor is He ever responsible for poor judgement.

This does not mean believers are left alone. God promises wisdom to those who ask, as we read in James 1:5, *"If any of you lacks wisdom, you should ask God, who gives generously to all without finding fault."* Wisdom is God's promised gift, not perfect foresight. When responsibility is embraced as part of God's design, decision-making becomes an arena for growth rather than fear.

Why the perfect choice mindset persists

Despite the Bible's clear teaching, the myth of the perfect choice persists because it offers emotional reassurance. If there is only one right option, then uncertainty feels less threatening. The problem is not uncertainty itself, but how it is interpreted.

The Bible never promises that life will be free of ambiguity. Instead, it promises God's presence within it. *"Surely I am with you always, to the very end of the age."* (Matthew 28:20). God's presence, not perfect clarity, is the foundation of all Christian confidence. The desire for perfect choices often reflects a deeper struggle with trust. Believers fear making decisions because they fear being alone in the outcome. The Bible answers this fear not with information, but with assurance. God does not abandon His people when they act in faith.

The limits the Bible places on choice

Recognising freedom does not mean denying limits. The Bible clearly defines boundaries for faithful living. Some choices are not available to believers because they contradict God's revealed will. Dishonesty, injustice, immorality, and unfaithfulness are never presented as legitimate options. Paul is very clear on this point: *"Do not be deceived: God cannot be mocked. A man reaps what he sows."* (Galatians 6:7).

Choices have consequences. Freedom does not cancel moral responsibility. Within those boundaries, however, the Bible allows real choice. Believers are called to choose wisely, not to wait indefinitely. They are invited to live actively rather than cautiously.

A shift that brings relief

When believers see the myth of the perfect choice, a noticeable shift occurs. Decisions become lighter, not because they are trivial, but because they are no longer burdened with impossible expectations. Faithfulness is no longer measured by accuracy, but by trust, obedience, and love. This shift does not lead to carelessness. It leads to attentiveness. Believers become more thoughtful, not less. They pray not for secret knowledge, but for wisdom. They seek counsel not to avoid responsibility, but to exercise it well.

The Bible invites believers into this freedom. *"Now the Lord is the Spirit, and where the Spirit of the Lord is, there is freedom."* (2 Corinthians 3:17). This freedom is not chaotic. It is purposeful. It is the freedom of those who know they are held securely within God's will, even as they make real decisions in a complex world. Understanding this is essential if confusion about God's will is to give way to confidence. God's will is not threatened by choice. It is honoured through faithful, responsible living before Him.

If the myth of the perfect choice undermines freedom, it also subtly distorts how believers understand God's involvement in their lives. Many Christians assume that if God is truly guiding them, He will make the right option unmistakably clear. When clarity does not come, they conclude that something is wrong. The Bible, however, presents God's involvement in a far richer and more relational way.

God's presence, not God's precision

One of the quiet assumptions behind anxiety-driven decision-making is the belief that God's guidance must always take the form of precision. Believers expect God to narrow their options until only one remains. Yet the Bible rarely portrays God's guidance in this way.

Instead, God repeatedly promises His presence rather than perfect information. When Moses expresses fear about leading Israel, God does not give him a detailed strategy for every challenge ahead. He reassures him with His presence: *"I will be with you."* (Exodus 3:12). The promise is relational, not logistical.

This pattern continues throughout the Bible. God's people are not given exhaustive direction. They are given assurance that God walks with them. David testifies in Psalm 23:4, *"Even though I walk through the darkest valley, I will fear no evil, for you are with me."*

Confidence rests not in knowing the path perfectly, but in knowing the Shepherd. When believers demand precision rather than presence, they often miss the form of guidance God has actually promised to give.

How trust grows through choice

Trust does not grow in the absence of choice. It grows through it. If every decision were predetermined and revealed in advance, trust would be unnecessary. Faith would just be reduced to compliance.

The Bible presents faith as something exercised, not bypassed. Abraham's story again illustrates this. God promises Abraham descendants and blessing, but He does not provide a step-by-step map of how events will unfold. Abraham is called to trust God's promise while navigating uncertainty. *"Abram believed the Lord, and he credited it to him as righteousness."* (Genesis 15:6).

This trust is not abstract. It is lived out in concrete decisions. Abraham acts, sometimes wisely, sometimes imperfectly, yet God always remains faithful. God's purposes are not undone by Abraham's limitations.

This narrative reassures believers that God's faithfulness does not depend on flawless decision-making. Choice, therefore, is not a threat to faith. It is one of the means by which faith is exercised and strengthened.

When responsibility feels too heavy

For too many believers, the idea of real responsibility feels overwhelming. The fear is not merely of choosing wrongly, but of bearing the consequences. Blueprint thinking often appeals precisely because it seems to shift responsibility back onto God. the Bible does not remove responsibility, but it reframes it.

Believers are not responsible for controlling outcomes. They are responsible for acting faithfully. Paul captures this balance when he writes, *"So we make it our goal to please him, whether we are at home in the body or away from it."* (2 Corinthians 5:9). The goal is faithfulness, not success.

This distinction is crucial. Faithfulness is within the believer's control. Outcomes are not. The Bible never holds believers accountable for results they could not foresee. It holds them accountable for obedience, integrity, and trust.

Jesus warns against anxious striving. *"Who of you by worrying can add a single hour to your life?"* (Matthew 6:27). Anxiety about outcomes accomplishes nothing. Trust in God's care frees believers to act responsibly without being crushed by fear.

God's will and consequences

Another fear that fuels the myth of the perfect choice is the belief that negative consequences always indicate a wrong decision. The Bible does not support this assumption. Faithful choices can lead to hardship, just as unwise choices can sometimes appear to succeed.

The apostle Paul's life is a striking example. His obedience repeatedly leads to suffering, imprisonment, and hardship. Yet he understands these experiences not as evidence of missing God's will, but as part of faithful service.

"I consider my life worth nothing to me; my only aim is to finish the race and complete the task the Lord Jesus has given me." (Acts 20:24). If consequences were the measure of God's will, Paul's life would make no sense.

The Bible instead measures faithfulness by obedience and trust, not by comfort or ease. This understanding protects believers from drawing false conclusions about their decisions. Difficulty does not automatically mean failure. Ease does not automatically mean success. God's will cannot be read off circumstances alone.

Learning from imperfect decisions

The Bible assumes that believers will sometimes make imperfect decisions. Growth comes not from avoiding mistakes at all costs, but from learning through experience. This learning is part of God's formative work.

Proverbs 1:5 affirms that wisdom grows over time. *"Let the wise listen and add to their learning."* Wisdom is cumulative. It develops as believers reflect on their choices and their outcomes in light of God's Word. God does not abandon His people when they choose imperfectly. He instead continues to teach, correct, and guide them. *"The Lord disciplines those he loves."* (Hebrews 12:6). Discipline is not punishment. It is formation.

This truth should bring us enormous relief. Believers are not expected to navigate life flawlessly. They are expected to remain teachable. God's will is not thwarted by growth that involves missteps.

Why the Bible encourages action

Throughout the Bible, there is a consistent bias toward action rather than paralysis. God's people are repeatedly urged to move forward in faith. *"Be strong and courageous. Do not be afraid; do not be discouraged."* (Joshua 1:9). Courage is needed precisely because certainty is not guaranteed.

Even in the New Testament, believers are encouraged to make plans while holding them humbly. James does not condemn planning. He condemns presumption. *"You ought to say, 'If it is the Lord's will, we will live and do this or that.'"*(James 4:15). The issue is not action, but attitude. The Bible calls believers to live with intention, wisdom, and trust.

Waiting is sometimes necessary, but hesitation born of fear is not commended. God's will is never honoured by indecision that springs from distrust.

A healthier way to approach decisions

When freedom, responsibility, and trust are held together, decision-making becomes a lot healthier. Believers pray not for perfect clarity, but for wisdom. They seek counsel not to avoid responsibility, but to exercise it well. They act not because they are certain, but because they trust God.

This approach reflects the Bible's own priorities. God's will is not a narrow path that must be located precisely. It is a broad call to faithful living within the boundaries He has revealed.

As believers learn how to release the myth of the perfect choice, anxiety will loosen its grip. Decisions become opportunities for growth rather than tests of spirituality. Confidence grows, not in one's own judgement, but in God's faithfulness. God's will is not threatened by choice. It is worked out through it, as believers live responsibly and trust deeply in the God who walks with them.

As the myth of the perfect choice begins to lose its grip, a deeper question often emerges: if God grants such freedom, how can believers be confident they are still living within His will? For many, the fear lingers that freedom might somehow place them outside God's care or beyond His purposes. The Bible addresses this fear directly and decisively.

God's will is bigger than our decisions

One of the most stabilising truths the Bible offers is that God's will is far larger than any individual decision. God's purposes are not narrow tracks that must be followed with precision. They are expansive realities that encompass human choice without being threatened by it.

Paul reassures believers of this when he writes, *"For those God foreknew he also predestined to be conformed to the image of his Son."* (Romans 8:29).

This verse does not focus on specific life decisions. It focuses on God's overarching purpose: transformation into Christlikeness. That purpose is not fragile. It is not easily derailed. It stands secure regardless of the twists and turns of individual lives.

When God's will is understood in terms of transformation rather than location or occupation, the fear of missing it begins to fade. Believers realise that God's will is being worked out through their lives, not held hostage by their choices.

Why the Bible does not obsess over outcomes

Another reason anxiety persists is that many believers measure God's will in terms of outcomes. Success is assumed to indicate faithfulness, while difficulty is assumed to signal error. The Bible consistently dismantles this way of thinking.

The lives of faithful believers in the Bible are marked by both triumph and suffering. Jeremiah obeys God faithfully and is rejected. The apostles proclaim the gospel and are persecuted. Jesus Himself is perfectly obedient and yet suffers unjustly. The Bible does not interpret these outcomes as evidence of failure. It interprets them as expressions of faithfulness in a fallen world.

Paul captures this perspective when he writes, *"We live by faith, not by sight."* (2 Corinthians 5:7). Faithfulness is not measured by visible results. It is measured by trust and obedience. God's will can never be reduced to a formula where the right choice will guarantee the right outcome.

When believers expect certain outcomes to confirm God's will, confusion is inevitable. The Bible calls believers to trust God's purposes even when outcomes are unclear or painful.

The security of God's commitment

Perhaps the greatest reassurance the Bible offers is that God is committed to His people far more deeply than they are to making the right choices. God's faithfulness does not fluctuate with human performance. It rests on His character.

Paul expresses this confidence with striking clarity: *"He who began a good work in you will carry it on to completion until the day of Christ Jesus."* (Philippians 1:6). God's work in believers is ongoing and guaranteed. It is not suspended while believers navigate decisions. It continues through them.

This promise radically alters how freedom is experienced. Believers are not walking a tightrope where one misstep leads to disaster. They are walking within the secure purposes of a faithful God. Responsibility remains real, but fear loses its power.

Freedom that deepens dependence

True Christian freedom does not lead to independence from God. It deepens dependence on Him. As believers exercise freedom and responsibility, they are continually driven back to prayer, the Bible, and community.

Prayer becomes less about asking God to choose for us and more about asking God to shape us. The psalmist prays, *"Teach me to do your will, for you are my God."* (Psalm 143:10). This prayer does not ask for specific instructions. It asks for formation. It reflects a desire to live rightly rather than to choose perfectly.

Community also plays a vital role. The Bible consistently places believers within the context of the church, where wisdom is shared and discernment is sharpened. *"As iron sharpens iron, so one person sharpens another."* (Proverbs 27:17). God often guides His people through the counsel and insight of others, not through private revelation. Freedom, rightly understood, draws believers into deeper relationship with God and with one another.

Living without the fear of regret

One of the quiet fears behind the myth of the perfect choice is regret. Believers fear looking back and realising they chose wrongly. The Bible addresses regret not by promising perfect foresight, but by affirming God's redeeming power.

Joel records God's promise to His people, *"I will repay you for the years the locusts have eaten."* (Joel 2:25). This promise speaks of restoration, not precision. God is able to redeem loss, failure, and misjudgement. The Christian life is not defined by regret, but by grace. Paul reflects this redemptive confidence, *"Forgetting what is behind and straining toward what is ahead, I press on toward the goal."* (Philippians 3:13–14). The focus is not on revisiting past decisions, but on continuing forward in faith. Believers are not called to live haunted by what might have been. They are called to live faithfully in the present, trusting God with both past and future.

A life anchored, not anxious

As the Bible dismantles the myth of the perfect choice, it replaces anxiety with assurance. Believers come to see that God's will is not something they can easily miss. It is something God is actively working out within them.

This does not make decisions unimportant. It places them in proper perspective. Choices matter, but they do not carry the weight of ultimate meaning. God's purposes are deeper and broader than any single decision.

The result is a life anchored rather than anxious. Believers are free to act, learn, and grow. They are secure in the knowledge that God is faithful and that His will is being accomplished as they walk with Him.

The Bible invites believers into this freedom. *"Cast all your anxiety on him because he cares for you."* (1 Peter 5:7). Anxiety thrives where trust is weak. Freedom flourishes where trust is strong.

When the myth of the perfect choice is finally set aside, God's will no longer appears as a narrow path that must be walked with fear. It appears as a secure calling to live faithfully, wisely, and confidently before a God whose purposes cannot fail.

5. GOD'S WILL IS A PERSON, NOT A PATH

Confusion about God's will has surely been fuelled by blueprint thinking and anxiety about perfect choices, but the Bible offers a far more relational and grounding vision. At the centre of God's will we don't find a path to be discovered - we find a person to be known. The Bible consistently directs attention away from abstract plans and toward the living reality of a relationship with God in Christ.

This shift is not subtle. It represents one of the most significant reorientations in how believers understand obedience, guidance, and faithfulness. God's will is not primarily something believers follow. It is someone they belong to.

God's will revealed in Christ

The New Testament is unmistakably Christ-centred in the way it speaks about God's will. God's purposes are not finally revealed in instructions or strategies, but in His Son. The writer to the Hebrews makes this explicit: *"In the past God spoke to our ancestors through the prophets at many times and in various ways, but in these last days he has spoken to us by his Son."* (Hebrews 1:1–2).

This statement marks a decisive and important shift. God's will is no longer progressively revealed through a series of messages. It is definitively revealed in a person. Jesus does not merely communicate God's will. He embodies it. To know Christ is to know the will of God in its fullest expression.

Jesus Himself affirms this when He declares, *"Anyone who has seen me has seen the Father."* (John 14:9). God's character, God's purposes, and God's heart and desires are not hidden behind complex discernment processes. They are made visible in the life, teaching, and self-giving love of Jesus.

When believers search for God's will apart from Jesus Christ, confusion is inevitable. The Bible consistently directs them back to Him as the centre of God's purposes.

Union with Christ changes everything

One of the most profound truths of the New Testament is that believers are united with Christ. This union is not metaphorical. It is spiritual and real. Believers do not merely follow Christ from a distance. They participate in His life.

Paul describes this union clearly in Galatians 2:20, *"I have been crucified with Christ and I no longer live, but Christ lives in me."* This union radically reshapes how God's will is understood. God's will is no longer external to the believer. God's will is worked out internally through the life of Christ within them.

Because believers are united with Christ, they are not attempting to align themselves with a distant plan. They are living from a shared life. God's will is not discovered by stepping into the right circumstance. It is expressed as Christ's life is formed within His people.

This truth dismantles the idea that God's will must be located in specific life paths. God's primary concern is not where believers go, but who they are becoming. Union with Christ ensures that God's will is always at work, regardless of circumstance.

Following Christ rather than finding direction

The Bible repeatedly frames the Christian life in terms of following Christ rather than finding direction. Jesus does not invite His disciples to analyse their future. He calls them to follow Him. *"Whoever wants to be my disciple must deny themselves and take up their cross daily and follow me."* (Luke 9:23).

This call is deliberately relational. Jesus does not provide His disciples with a detailed roadmap. He provides Himself. The focus is not on knowing the destination, but on trusting the One who leads.

When believers replace following Christ with seeking guidance, priorities are then very subtly reversed. Instead of attending to relationship, they fixate on outcomes. Instead of walking with Christ, they wait for clarity. The Bible consistently calls believers to the opposite posture.

Jesus reassures His disciples, *"My sheep listen to my voice; I know them, and they follow me."* (John 10:27). This following is not primarily about receiving instructions. It is about recognising and trusting the Shepherd.

Why this relieves so much pressure

Understanding God's will as personal rather than procedural brings immense relief. Believers are no longer burdened with the responsibility of deciphering God's intentions. They are freed to focus on knowing and trusting Christ.

This does not trivialise decisions. It reframes them. Choices are made within a relationship rather than as tests of spiritual accuracy. Believers ask not, "Have I found the right path?" but, "Am I walking with Christ in this?"

Paul captures this relational orientation when he writes, *"For me, to live is Christ."* (Philippians 1:21). God's will is not something added to life. It is life centred on Christ. When Christ is central, decision-making becomes an extension of discipleship rather than a separate spiritual exercise. Believers seek to honour Christ in whatever they do, trusting that His life within them is shaping their desires and actions.

God's will expressed through Christlike living

The Bible consistently connects God's will with Christlike living. When the Bible explicitly states what God's will is, it does so in relational and moral terms. Believers are called to reflect the character of Christ.

Paul writes, *"Follow God's example, therefore, as dearly loved children and walk in the way of love, just as Christ loved us and gave himself up for us."* (Ephesians 5:1–2). God's will is not hidden here. It is plainly stated. It is expressed through love shaped by Christ's self-giving.

Similarly, Peter reminds believers, *"Just as he who called you is holy, so be holy in all you do."* (1 Peter 1:15). Holiness is not tied to particular circumstances. It is a way of living that flows from belonging to Christ.

These commands are comprehensive and demanding, yet they do not require special insight. They are lived out wherever believers find themselves. God's will is not confined to particular decisions. It permeates everyday life.

From anxiety to abiding

When God's will is understood as a person rather than a path or procedure, anxiety begins to lose its grip. Believers are no longer preoccupied with getting somewhere. They are concerned with abiding in Christ. Our Lord invites His disciples into this posture: *"Remain in me, as I also remain in you. No branch can bear fruit by itself; it must remain in the vine."* (John 15:4).

Fruitfulness flows not from correct navigation, but from abiding relationship. This imagery is powerful. Branches do not search for direction. They remain connected. Fruit appears not because the branch knows what to do, but because it shares the life of the vine. God's will is fulfilled not through anxious striving, but through faithful abiding.

When believers grasp this, the Christian life takes on a totally different tone. Trust replaces fear. Presence replaces precision. Relationship replaces technique. God's will is then no longer something to chase. It is something to live within as believers walk with Christ day by day.

If God's will is fundamentally personal rather than procedural, then obedience itself must be understood relationally. The Bible consistently presents obedience not as the execution of certain instructions, but as the response of love to a Person. This is one of the most liberating truths in the New Testament, yet it is often overshadowed by an overly mechanical view of guidance.

Obedience flowing from relationship

Jesus makes it clear that obedience flows out of relationship, not fear or obligation. On the night before His crucifixion, He tells His disciples, *"If you love me, keep my commands."* (John 14:15). The order matters. Love comes first. Obedience follows. Jesus does not say, "If you want to know my will, then keep my commands." He says obedience is the natural expression of love for Him.

This relational framework reshapes how God's will is lived out. Obedience is not an anxious attempt to remain in God's favour. It is the response of those who already belong. Jesus reinforces this when He says, *"As the Father has loved me, so have I loved you. Now remain in my love."* (John 15:9). Remaining precedes doing. Belonging precedes obedience.

When believers decide to reverse this order, obedience becomes burdensome. When they keep it intact, obedience becomes life-giving. God's will is no longer a list of expectations to meet, but a relationship to honour.

Knowing Christ shapes desire

One of the great promises of the New Covenant is that God works not only on behaviour, but on desire. As believers grow in their knowledge of Christ, their wants begin to change. God's will becomes less about resisting temptation and more about delighting in what honours Him.

The psalmist expresses this beautifully: *"Take delight in the Lord, and he will give you the desires of your heart."* (Psalm 37:4). This verse is often misunderstood as a promise that God will grant whatever believers want. In context, it speaks of transformation. As delight in the Lord grows, desires are reshaped to reflect His heart.

Paul echoes this truth when he writes in Philippians 2:13, *"For it is God who works in you to will and to act in order to fulfil his good purpose."* God's work reaches into the will itself. Believers are not left to battle competing desires alone. God is actively forming new ones within them.

This explains why the Bible places such emphasis on knowing Christ. Knowledge here is not merely intellectual. It is relational and transformative. The more believers know Christ, the more their instincts align with His.

Guidance through formation rather than instruction

When God's will is understood relationally, guidance is no longer expected primarily in the form of instructions. Instead, it is experienced through formation.

God guides His people by shaping who they are, not by telling them what to do at every turn.

Paul prays for this kind of growth when he asks that believers may be *"filled with the knowledge of his will through all the wisdom and understanding that the Spirit gives."* (Colossians 1:9). Notice how knowledge of God's will is connected to wisdom and understanding, not to specific directives. It is the kind of knowledge that produces a way of life.

As believers are shaped by Christ, they increasingly recognise what fits and what does not. Decisions are guided by character. Choices flow from identity. God's will is discerned not by consulting a map, but by walking as someone who belongs to Christ. This kind of guidance is quieter than many expect, but it is far more stable. It does not depend on emotional intensity or dramatic experiences. It grows steadily through the Bible, prayer, and faithful living.

Freedom to choose within a living relationship

A relational understanding of God's will also affirms genuine freedom. Believers are not merely actors following a script. They are participants in a living relationship. God delights in their obedience, but He also honours their agency.

Paul addresses this freedom directly in 1 Corinthians 10:31, *"So whether you eat or drink or whatever you do, do it all for the glory of God."* This exhortation assumes that believers will make many decisions not specified in the Bible. The focus is not on which option is chosen, but on the spirit in which it is chosen.

Freedom within relationship does not weaken obedience. It deepens it. Believers choose not because they must, but because they want to honour Christ. God's will is not imposed externally. It is embraced internally.

This also explains why the Bible allows diversity in non-essential matters. Believers may make different choices without violating God's will, as long as those choices are shaped by love, faith, and obedience. God's will is not threatened by variety. It is expressed through faithfulness.

The role of love in discerning God's will

Love is one of the most reliable guides in discerning God's will. The Bible repeatedly connects love with fulfilment of God's purposes. Paul writes, *"The only thing that counts is faith expressing itself through love."* (Galatians 5:6). Faith is not abstract. It is active and relational.

When believers ask whether a decision aligns with God's will, one of the most searching questions they can ask is whether it expresses love. Does it reflect love for God and love for others? Does it build up, serve, and honour?

This does not reduce God's will to sentiment. Biblical love is shaped by truth and holiness. But it provides a powerful lens through which decisions can be evaluated. God's will is not found by escaping love in pursuit of certainty. It is found by walking in love shaped by Christ.

Resting in the faithfulness of Christ

Perhaps the greatest freedom that comes from understanding God's will as personal is the freedom to rest. Believers are no longer striving to locate the right path. They are trusting the right Person.

Jesus invites His followers into this rest when He says, *"Come to me, all you who are weary and burdened, and I will give you rest."* (Matthew 11:28). The burden He lifts is not merely moral guilt. It is the weight of trying to manage life apart from trust in Him.

When Christ is central, God's will is no longer something to be solved. It is something to be lived. Decisions are made in prayerful dependence, but without crippling fear. Believers rest not in their ability to choose correctly, but in Christ's faithfulness.

This rest does not produce passivity. It produces confidence. Believers act, decide, and move forward, trusting that Christ is at work in them and through them. God's will is not a destination to reach. It is a relationship to inhabit.

As this truth takes hold, the Christian life becomes less about navigating uncertainty and more about walking faithfully with Christ, confident that His life within them is shaping every step they take.

When God's will is understood in these terms, the entire shape of the Christian life is reframed. The focus shifts from managing decisions to cultivating faithfulness, from mastering guidance techniques to deepening communion with Christ. This shift does not make the Christian life vague or directionless. It gives it a far clearer centre.

Abiding as the heart of God's will

Jesus' teaching about abiding captures the essence of how God's will is lived out. *"Remain in me, as I also remain in you. No branch can bear fruit by itself; it must remain in the vine."* (John 15:4). Fruitfulness flows from connection, not calculation. The branch does not strategise about where to grow fruit. It just remains connected, and fruit follows naturally.

This imagery is decisive. God's will is not about choosing correctly between certain options. It is about remaining faithfully connected to Christ. As believers abide in Him, their lives begin to bear fruit that reflects God's purposes. Obedience, wisdom, and discernment flow from relationship, not from technique. This also explains why the Bible places such emphasis on perseverance. Abiding is not a momentary experience. It is a settled posture. Faithfulness over time matters more than momentary clarity. God's will is not discovered in flashes of insight but lived out through enduring relationship.

Fruit as evidence, not strategy

The Bible consistently presents fruit as evidence of God's work, not as something believers manufacture. Jesus says, *"By their fruit you will recognise them."* (Matthew 7:16)

Fruit reveals what is already taking place internally. It is not the result of perfect planning, but of healthy connection. Paul lists the fruit of the Spirit as qualities that emerge from life in Christ: *"love, joy, peace, forbearance, kindness, goodness, faithfulness, gentleness and self-control."* (Galatians 5:22–23)

None of these are tied to specific circumstances. They can flourish in any setting. God's will is not limited to particular roles or environments. It is expressed wherever Christ's life is present.

When believers evaluate their lives primarily by whether they feel certain about decisions, they may miss the deeper evidence of God's work. The Bible invites them to look instead at fruit.

Is love growing?

Is faith being strengthened?

Is patience deepening?

These are far more reliable indicators of alignment with God's will than circumstantial clarity.

How this shapes everyday decisions

Understanding God's will as personal does not eliminate the need to make decisions. It reshapes how those decisions are approached. Believers no longer ask, "Which option guarantees I am in God's will?" They ask, "How can I honour Christ in this situation?"

This question is both simpler and more demanding. It cannot be answered by a formula. It requires attentiveness to the Bible, sensitivity to conscience, and awareness of others. It draws believers into active engagement rather than passive waiting.

Paul encourages this posture when he writes, *"Whatever you do, work at it with all your heart, as working for the Lord, not for human masters."* (Colossians 3:23).

This exhortation assumes that believers will be doing many things not specified by the Bible. God's will is honoured not by the nature of the task, but by the heart with which it is done.
This approach also guards against regret.

When decisions are made prayerfully and faithfully, believers can entrust outcomes to God. Even when circumstances are difficult, they can rest in the knowledge that they sought to honour Christ. God's will is not undone by imperfect outcomes.

God's will and the ordinary faithfulness of life

One of the quiet dangers of misunderstanding God's will is the assumption that it must be dramatic. Believers may feel that unless their lives involve very clear callings or extraordinary guidance, they are missing something. The Bible challenges this assumption.

Much of the New Testament addresses ordinary faithfulness: working honestly, loving family, serving others, persevering in hardship. Paul urges believers to *"lead a quiet life, to mind your own business and to work with your hands."* (1 Thessalonians 4:11). This is not a diminished vision of God's will. It is a realistic one.

God's will is so often expressed most clearly in the ordinary rhythms of life. Faithfulness in small things matters. Integrity in daily choices matters. Love in unseen places matters. These are not distractions from God's will. They are its substance. When believers really grasp this, the pressure to find something extraordinary lifts. They are free to live fully and faithfully where they are, trusting that God is at work in ordinary obedience.

Confidence rooted in relationship

Perhaps the greatest gift of understanding God's will as personal is confidence. This confidence does not come from knowing the future. It comes from knowing Christ. Believers are assured that as they walk with Him, they are living within God's will.

John expresses this assurance when he writes, *"This is how we know that we live in him and he in us: He has given us of his Spirit."* (1 John 4:13). God's Spirit is not given to enable perfect decision-making, but to sustain faithful relationship. Only then will they no longer live under the constant anxiety of missing God's will. They will live with the quiet assurance that God is at work in them, shaping their lives according to His purposes.

From seeking to trusting

So the shift now becomes very clear. God's will is not something believers must endlessly seek. It is something they are invited to trust.

Trusting does not mean ignoring wisdom or counsel. It means placing those things within the larger context of relationship with Christ.

The Bible consistently invites believers into this trust. *"Commit your way to the Lord; trust in him and he will do this."* (Psalm 37:5). The promise is not that God will reveal every detail, but that He will be faithful as believers entrust their lives to Him.

When God's will is understood as personal, the Christian life takes on a steadier rhythm. Believers walk, decide, and grow with confidence, knowing that their lives are held securely in Christ. God's will is not a path that must be located with precision. It is a relationship that sustains and shapes believers as they live faithfully before Him.

In this light, confusion gives way to clarity, anxiety to trust, and striving to rest. God's will is no longer an elusive concept. It is the lived reality of walking with Christ, day by day, in faithful dependence on the One who has already revealed Himself fully and finally.

6. LIVING WITHIN GOD'S WILL RATHER THAN SEARCHING FOR IT

One of the quiet but powerful shifts that will take place when believers rethink God's will from a biblical perspective is the movement from *searching* to *living*. For many Christians, God's will has been treated as something ahead of them, something to be located before life can properly move forward. The Bible, however, consistently presents God's will as something believers already inhabit as they live by faith in Christ. This shift does not minimise the importance of wisdom or prayer. It restores them to their proper place. God's will is not a destination reached by correct navigation. It is the sphere in which believers live as they walk with God.

God's will as the environment of faithful living

The Bible repeatedly portrays believers as already living within the will and purposes of God. Paul writes, *"In him we live and move and have our being."* (Acts 17:28). This statement does not describe a rare spiritual state. It describes the basic reality of human existence under God's sovereignty, and all the more so the reality of those who belong to Christ.

Believers are not stepping in and out of God's will as they make decisions. They are living within it as redeemed people. God's will is not a narrow line that must be followed perfectly. It is the secure framework of God's purposes within which faithful living takes place.

This is why the Bible can speak with such confidence about God's ongoing work in every believer's life. Paul wrote, *"For it is God who works in you to will and to act in order to fulfil his good purpose."* (Philippians 2:13). God's work is never paused while believers deliberate. It is continuous. God's will is being carried out as believers live, choose, and grow.

When this is understood, much of the anxiety surrounding decision-making begins to ease. Believers are no longer afraid of stepping outside God's will. They begin to recognise that God's will is actively shaping them from within.

Why the Bible emphasises walking rather than finding

The dominant metaphor the Bible uses for the Christian life is walking. Believers are called to walk by faith, walk in the Spirit, walk in love, and walk in the light. These images are significant. Walking implies movement, direction, and progress, but not full visibility of the road ahead.

Paul exhorts believers, *"Since we live by the Spirit, let us keep in step with the Spirit."* (Galatians 5:25). Keeping in step with the Spirit does not require knowing the entire route ahead of us. It requires attentiveness and responsiveness in the present moment. God's will is lived out step by step, not mapped out in advance.

Similarly, Paul writes in 2 Corinthians 5:7, *"For we live by faith, not by sight."* Genuine faith does not demand comprehensive understanding. It trusts God's faithfulness as life unfolds. The insistence on seeing the whole path before acting is not an expression of faith, but a resistance to it.

The Bible consistently encourages believers to walk forward rather than wait for certainty. God's will is experienced through faithful movement, not static analysis.

The danger of treating God's will as a location

A great deal of confusion arises when God's will is treated as a location rather than a way of living. Believers speak of being "in" or "out of" God's will as though it were a place one could enter or leave. This language subtly reshapes how God's will is understood.

The Bible never uses this language in relation to everyday decisions. Instead, it speaks of living in obedience, walking in truth, and abiding in Christ. God's will is not presented as a place to reach, but as a relationship to live within.

Paul reminds believers, *"Therefore, as God's chosen people, holy and dearly loved, clothe yourselves with compassion, kindness, humility, gentleness and patience."* (Colossians 3:12). This exhortation assumes believers are already within God's purposes.

The call is not to get into God's will, but to live consistently with who they are in Christ. When God's will is treated as a location, believers become anxious about crossing invisible boundaries. When it is understood as a way of living, they become attentive to faithfulness in the present.

God's will and the ordinary flow of life

Another reason believers struggle with God's will is the assumption that it must always involve major decisions or dramatic moments. The Bible presents a much quieter picture. God's will is most often expressed through ordinary obedience in ordinary circumstances.

Paul instructs believers, *"Whatever you do, whether in word or deed, do it all in the name of the Lord Jesus."* (Colossians 3:17). This verse deliberately embraces the ordinary. God's will is not confined to special callings or pivotal moments. It encompasses everyday speech, work, and relationships.

Similarly, Peter urges believers in 1 Peter 2:12 to: *"Live such good lives among the pagans that... they may see your good deeds and glorify God."* God's will is worked out in visible faithfulness over time, not in isolated moments of guidance.

When believers fixate on finding God's will for the future, they all too often neglect living God's will in the present. The Bible consistently calls them back to faithful obedience now.

The stability this brings to decision-making

Understanding God's will as something believers live within rather than search for, will bring stability to decision-making. Decisions are no longer treated as moments of spiritual danger. They are treated as expressions of faithfulness within God's care. This does not remove the need for wisdom or prayer. It places them in context. Believers pray not because God's will is absent, but because they want to live wisely within it. They seek counsel not because they fear being outside God's will, but because they desire to honour God in their choices.

James captures this posture when he writes, *"If it is the Lord's will, we will live and do this or that."* (James 4:15). This statement reflects humility, not hesitation. Plans are made. Life moves forward. God's sovereignty is acknowledged without paralysing action.

Freedom from the fear of missing God's will

Perhaps the greatest gift of this perspective is freedom from the fear of missing God's will. The Bible never suggests that God's will is easily missed by sincere believers. On the contrary, it repeatedly affirms God's faithfulness in leading His people.

The psalmist declares, *"The Lord makes firm the steps of the one who delights in him."* (Psalm 37:23). God's guidance is not dependent on perfect discernment. It flows from relationship. God directs those who delight in Him, even as they take imperfect steps. This assurance does not encourage carelessness. It encourages trust. Believers are freed to live actively and responsibly, confident that God is at work in their lives.

From searching to faithful living

When the search for God's will gives way to faithful living within it, the Christian life takes on a steadier rhythm. Believers stop treating life as a series of tests to pass and begin living it as a relationship to enjoy and honour.

God's will is not discovered by standing still. It is lived out as believers walk by faith, guided by the Bible, shaped by Christ, and sustained by grace. This understanding does not answer every question about the future. It does something better. It anchors believers in the present, where God is already at work.

In this light, God's will no longer feels elusive or fragile. It is the secure context in which believers live, grow, and learn to trust the God who is faithful in every step they take.

Once believers grasp that God's will is something they live within rather than hunt for, the posture of prayer and discernment begins to change. Prayer no longer functions as a way of extracting information from God, but as a means of alignment with Him. This shift brings both clarity and peace.

Prayer as alignment, not information gathering

Many Christians approach prayer primarily as a way of asking God to reveal His will. They ask for signs, clarity, or confirmation before acting. While the Bible encourages believers to pray about everything, it does not present prayer as a mechanism for discovering hidden instructions.

Jesus' own teaching on prayer reflects this orientation. In the Lord's Prayer, He teaches His disciples to pray, *"Your will be done, on earth as it is in heaven."* (Matthew 6:10). This is not a request for information. It is a posture of submission and trust. The prayer assumes that God's will is already established and good, and that the believer's life is to be aligned with it.

Prayer, then, is less about learning what God wants and more about being shaped to want what God wants. As believers pray, their hearts are reordered, their priorities clarified, and their anxieties quieted.

The Bible as the primary guide

When God's will is understood as something believers can live within, the Bible takes on its proper role as the primary guide for faithful living. The Bible is not a collection of clues pointing toward hidden plans. It is God's revealed will, sufficient for life and godliness.

Paul reminds Timothy, *"All the Bible is God-breathed and is useful for teaching, rebuking, correcting and training in righteousness, so that the servant of God may be thoroughly equipped for every good work."* (2 Timothy 3:16–17). The Bible equips believers not by providing detailed instructions for every scenario, but by forming them to live faithfully in whatever circumstances they face. God's will is not hidden beyond the Bible. It is revealed through it.

This is why the Bible is described as sufficient. Peter writes that God's divine power *"has given us everything we need for a godly life through our knowledge of him who called us."* (2 Peter 1:3). If the Bible truly provides everything needed for godly living, then believers are not lacking essential information about God's will. What they need most is not additional guidance, but faithful application of what has already been given.

Therefore, when the Bible is treated as foundational rather than supplementary, much confusion fades. Believers are no longer scanning the Bible for personalised instructions. They are allowing the Bible to shape their thinking, values, and priorities.

Wisdom applied in real time

Living within God's will requires wisdom applied in real time. Wisdom bridges the gap between the Bible and everyday life. It enables believers to discern how God's revealed will takes shape in specific situations.

The Bible places extraordinary emphasis on wisdom. *"The fear of the Lord is the beginning of wisdom."* (Proverbs 9:10). Wisdom grows out of reverent trust in God, not out of access to secret knowledge. It develops as believers live attentively before God, learning through experience and reflection.

James reinforces this when he urges believers to ask God for wisdom rather than direction. *"If any of you lacks wisdom, you should ask God, who gives generously to all without finding fault."* (James 1:5). Wisdom is promised. Detailed instructions are not. This distinction matters. God delights to form wise people rather than micromanage their decisions.

Wisdom also involves recognising that faithful believers may make different choices in similar circumstances. The Bible allows for this diversity. God's will is never undermined by faithful disagreement. It is expressed through lives shaped by truth and love.

The role of conscience

Conscience plays a vital role in living within God's will. The Bible treats conscience as something that can be trained and strengthened. Paul speaks of *"a clear conscience before God and man."* (Acts 24:16). A well-formed conscience helps believers navigate decisions the Bible does not explicitly address.

Conscience, however, is not autonomous. It must be shaped by the Bible and community. Paul warns against consciences that are weak or misinformed (1 Corinthians 8:7).

This means believers must remain teachable, willing to have their assumptions corrected. Living within God's will does not mean trusting instinct alone. It means allowing conscience to be formed by God's Word and guided by love for others. When conscience is exercised humbly and thoughtfully, it becomes a reliable ally in faithful decision-making.

Counsel and community as God's provision

The Bible consistently presents community as one of God's primary means of guidance. God's will is not meant to be discerned in isolation. Wisdom is always sharpened through relationship.

Proverbs 20:18 reminds us, *"Plans fail for lack of counsel, but with many advisers they succeed."* This proverb assumes that decisions are being made. It does not assume perfect clarity beforehand. Counsel helps believers test their thinking, expose blind spots, and gain perspective.

The New Testament reinforces this communal orientation. Believers are called to *"encourage one another and build each other up."* (1 Thessalonians 5:11). God often guides His people through the insight and wisdom of others rather than through private revelation.

This does not diminish personal responsibility. It strengthens it. Seeking counsel is an expression of humility, not indecision. It reflects a recognition that God works through His people together.

Acting in faith rather than waiting for certainty

Living within God's will often requires acting without full certainty. The Bible never portrays this as irresponsible. It portrays it as faith. Faith does not wait until all questions are answered. It moves forward trusting God's character.

Paul's ministry offers a clear example. He frequently makes plans while acknowledging their provisional nature. *"I plan to do so when I go to Spain."* (Romans 15:28). He plans, acts, and trusts God with the outcome. There is no hint of anxiety about missing God's will.

In James 4:14, believers are cautioned against presumption, not against planning. *"You do not even know what will happen tomorrow."* (James 4:14). This humility does not lead to paralysis. It leads to trustful action. God's will is honoured not by avoiding decisions, but by holding them before God as they are made.

The peace that comes from trust

One of the marks of living within God's will is peace. This peace does not arise from certainty, but from trust. Paul exhorts believers, *"Do not be anxious about anything, but in every situation, by prayer and petition, with thanksgiving, present your requests to God."* (Philippians 4:6). The promise that then follows is quite striking: *"And the peace of God... will guard your hearts and your minds in Christ Jesus."* (Philippians 4:7).

Notice that peace is what is promised, not clarity. God does not guarantee that every decision will feel clear. He promises peace that guards the heart as believers trust Him. This peace enables action without fear.

When believers live within God's will rather than searching for it, anxiety begins to loosen its grip. They are no longer driven by the need to be certain. They are sustained by the confidence that God is faithful.

A steady, faithful way of life

Living within God's will produces a steady, faithful way of life. Believers pray, read the Bible, seek counsel, and act responsibly. They learn from experience. They grow in wisdom. They trust God with outcomes they cannot control.

God's will is not something they enter and exit. It is the secure context of their lives in Christ. The Bible invites believers into this stability again and again. *"The Lord will watch over your coming and going both now and forevermore."* (Psalm 121:8).

This assurance frees believers to live fully and faithfully. God's will is not elusive or fragile. It is the gracious environment in which God's people live, choose, and grow as they walk with Him day by day.

As believers grow accustomed to living within God's will rather than searching for it, a deeper confidence begins to settle. Life is no longer experienced as a series of spiritual tests, each one threatening to derail God's purposes. Instead, it becomes a faithful journey which is marked by trust, obedience, and steady dependence on God's grace.

God's faithfulness over time

One of the most reassuring truths the Bible offers is that God's faithfulness extends over time, not just moments. God is not only present at key decision points. He is present throughout the whole of life. The psalmist declares, *"The Lord will keep you from all harm – he will watch over your life."* (Psalm 121:7). This promise does not expire once a decision is made. It continues as life unfolds.

Paul expresses similar confidence when he writes, *"The Lord is faithful, and he will strengthen you and protect you from the evil one."* (2 Thessalonians 3:3). God's faithfulness does not depend on perfect judgement. It rests on His character. Believers are sustained not by their ability to choose correctly, but by God's commitment to them.

This long-term faithfulness reframes how past decisions are viewed. Regret loses its sting when believers trust that God has been at work all along, even through uncertainty, weakness, and imperfect choices.

Learning through the journey

The Bible always assumes that growth happens through lived experience. Believers are not shaped merely by instruction, but by walking through life with God. This includes learning through success and failure alike.

Paul acknowledges this process when he writes, *"Not that I have already obtained all this, or have already arrived at my goal, but I press on."* (Philippians 3:12). Growth is progressive. It unfolds over time. God's will is not fulfilled in a single moment of clarity, but through ongoing transformation.

This perspective frees believers from the burden of perfection. They are not expected to navigate life without missteps. They are expected to remain responsive, teachable, and faithful. God uses even flawed experiences to deepen wisdom and maturity.

The promise of Romans remains steady throughout this whole process: *"In all things God works for the good of those who love him"* (Romans 8:28). This does not mean every choice leads to immediate good. It means God is able to work redemptively through all of life.

God's will and the shape of our life

Living within God's will gradually shapes the overall direction of a believer's whole life. Rather than being defined by isolated decisions, life is marked by consistent patterns of faithfulness. The Bible repeatedly calls believers to this kind of steady obedience.

Micah summarises God's desire succinctly: *"What does the Lord require of you? To act justly and to love mercy and to walk humbly with your God."* (Micah 6:8). This is not a checklist for specific decisions. It is a description of a way of life. God's will is embodied in how believers walk with Him day by day.

Similarly, Paul urges believers to *"live a life worthy of the calling you have received."* (Ephesians 4:1). This calling is not tied to a particular role or circumstance. It is expressed through character, humility, patience, and love. When believers focus on these enduring qualities, the pressure which surrounds individual decisions diminishes. God's will is seen not as fragile or elusive, but as deeply woven into the fabric of daily life.

Stability in an uncertain world

Living within God's will does not remove uncertainty from life. The Bible never promises that believers will be spared confusion, loss, pain or hardship. What it does promises is stability within uncertainty. Isaiah captures this assurance when he writes, *"You will keep in perfect peace those whose minds are steadfast, because they trust in you."* (Isaiah 26:3).

Peace flows from trust, not from control. Believers are anchored not by certainty about the future, but by confidence in God's faithfulness.

Jesus reinforces this stability when He compares those who hear and act on His words to a house built on rock. *"The rain came down, the streams rose, and the winds blew and beat against that house; yet it did not fall."* (Matthew 7:25). The house still faces storms. Stability comes from foundation, not avoidance. God's will provides this foundation. It is not a fragile path easily lost, but a secure reality rooted in God's unchanging purposes.

Freedom to live fully

Perhaps the most liberating outcome of living within God's will is the freedom to live fully. Believers are no longer constrained by fear of making the wrong move. They are free to love, serve, work, and rest with confidence.

Paul encourages this freedom when he writes, *"Whatever happens, conduct yourselves in a manner worthy of the gospel of Christ."* (Philippians 1:27). This exhortation assumes flexibility. Life may unfold in unexpected ways, but faithfulness remains possible in every circumstance.

This freedom does not produce carelessness. It produces engagement. Believers invest themselves fully in the life God has given them, trusting that He is present and at work.

A life entrusted to God

Ultimately, living within God's will is an act of trust. It is the recognition that life belongs to God and is held securely in His hands. Believers are invited to entrust not only their decisions, but their entire lives to Him.

Peter captures this posture when he writes, *"Those who suffer according to God's will, should commit themselves to their faithful Creator and continue to do good."* (1 Peter 4:19).

Commitment and action go together. Trust does not lead to withdrawal, but to perseverance.

As believers learn to live within God's will rather than searching for it, the Christian life becomes steadier and more joyful.

Anxiety gives way to trust.

Paralysis gives way to faithful action.

Confusion gives way to clarity rooted in relationship with God.

God's will is not something so fragile that it must be constantly protected. It is the gracious, sustaining purpose of a faithful God who walks with His people through every season of life.

Living within that will, believers find not only direction, but peace, confidence, and freedom as they journey onward in faith.

7. GUIDANCE, WISDOM, AND THE ROLE OF THE HOLY SPIRIT

As believers grow in confidence that God's will is something they live within rather than search for, an important question naturally arises: what, then, is the role of the Holy Spirit in guidance?

Many Christians assume that the Spirit's primary function is to provide direction for decisions. The Bible presents a richer and more profound picture. The Holy Spirit is given not to replace wisdom, but to form it.

The Spirit given to transform, not to replace thinking

One of the most common misunderstandings about the Holy Spirit is the idea that His guidance bypasses human thought. Believers may expect the Spirit to supply impressions, inner voices, or unmistakable prompts that remove the need for judgement. The Bible consistently resists this expectation.

Paul describes the Spirit's work as transformative rather than directive. *"Do not conform to the pattern of this world, but be transformed by the renewing of your mind."* (Romans 12:2).

The Spirit renews the mind. He does not suspend it. God's will is discerned through transformed thinking, not through the absence of thinking.

This is a crucial distinction. The Spirit does not guide believers by turning them into passive recipients of instruction. He guides them by reshaping how they perceive reality.

As minds are renewed, believers become increasingly able to recognise what aligns with God's character and purposes.

This explains why the Bible places such emphasis on maturity. Believers are expected to grow in discernment. *"The person with the Spirit makes judgements about all things."* (1 Corinthians 2:15). The Spirit enables judgement; He does not eliminate it.

The Spirit and the Word working together

The Bible never separates the work of the Spirit from the Word of God. The Spirit inspired the Bible, and He continues to illuminate that text. Guidance that claims to come from the Spirit but contradicts the Bible is immediately suspect.

Jesus promises His disciples that the Spirit will guide them into truth: *"When he, the Spirit of truth, comes, he will guide you into all the truth."* (John 16:13). In context, this guidance is closely tied to Jesus' teaching. The Spirit does not introduce new revelation about personal plans. He deepens understanding of what God has already revealed in Christ.

This is why the early church devoted itself to the apostles' teaching alongside prayer and fellowship (Acts 2:42). The Spirit worked through the Word to shape the community's life. Guidance emerged as the Bible was taught, believed, and lived. When believers look to the Spirit for guidance apart from the Bible, confusion follows. When they allow the Spirit to work through the Bible, clarity grows. God's will is not revealed by bypassing the Word, but by being shaped by it.

Why the Spirit is not a personal navigator

Popular Christian language often treats the Holy Spirit as a kind of personal navigator, offering turn-by-turn directions for life. While this imagery can be comforting, it does not reflect how the Bible describes the Spirit's ministry.

The New Testament rarely depicts the Holy Spirit giving specific instructions about the day-to-day decisions of life. Instead, the Spirit empowers obedience, produces fruit, and strengthens believers to live faithfully. *"Walk by the Spirit, and you will not gratify the desires of the flesh."* (Galatians 5:16). The promise here is moral transformation, not logistical guidance.

When the Spirit does intervene directly, it is usually in matters directly related to the advance of the gospel or the mission of the church. Even then, such moments are exceptional rather than normative. They certainly do not establish a pattern for everyday decision-making.

The Bible's emphasis remains consistent. The Spirit's primary role is to conform believers to Christ. Guidance flows out of that transformation rather than replacing it.

Wisdom as the Spirit's ordinary tool

If the Spirit does not generally provide direct instructions, how does He guide? The Bible's answer is clear: through wisdom. Wisdom is the Spirit-shaped capacity to live faithfully in complex situations.

Paul prays that believers may receive *"the Spirit of wisdom and revelation."* (Ephesians 1:17). This wisdom is not a kind of secret knowledge. It is insight into God's purposes and character. It enables believers to see life from God's perspective.

Wisdom involves applying God's truth thoughtfully. It requires attention, humility, and patience. It grows as believers engage the Bible, reflect on experience, and remain open to correction. The Spirit is active throughout this process, shaping judgement and sharpening discernment. This understanding will protect believers from two extremes. It prevents them from expecting constant supernatural direction, and it prevents them from relying solely on their own reasoning. Wisdom is neither mystical nor merely rational. It is Spirit-formed.

The fruit of the Spirit as guidance

One of the clearest ways the Spirit guides believers is through the fruit He produces in their lives. These qualities shape how decisions are made and how situations are approached. *"The fruit of the Spirit is love, joy, peace, forbearance, kindness, goodness, faithfulness, gentleness and self-control."* (Galatians 5:22–23).

A person growing in these qualities will naturally make different choices from someone driven by fear, pride, or impulse. Love influences priorities. Peace always steadies judgement. Self-control restrains rash action. These fruits function as guides, even though they are rarely recognised as such. The Bible does not present guidance as separate from character. It flows from it. As the Spirit produces Christlike character, believers become increasingly equipped to live within God's will.

From dependence to maturity

Understanding the Spirit's role in guidance moves believers from dependence toward real maturity. Dependence is not abandoned. It is deepened. Believers depend on the Spirit not to choose for them, but to shape them.

Paul describes this growth when he writes, *"Those who are led by the Spirit of God are the children of God."* (Romans 8:14). Being led by the Spirit does not mean being told what to do at every step. It means living as those whose lives are shaped by God's presence within them.

As this truth settles, believers are then freed from unrealistic expectations. They stop demanding constant direction and begin cultivating wisdom. They stop waiting for signs and start living faithfully. The Spirit is honoured not by passivity, but by responsiveness.

In this way, the Holy Spirit's guidance becomes both quieter and more profound. It is not dramatic or attention-grabbing. It is steady, faithful, and deeply transformative. God's will is lived out as the Spirit shapes believers from the inside, enabling them to walk wisely and confidently before God in every season of life.

If the Holy Spirit primarily guides by shaping wisdom rather than supplying instructions, this raises an important question: how should believers understand experiences that feel like guidance? Many Christians can point to moments when they sensed a strong impression, felt compelled toward a particular course of action, or experienced unusual clarity. The Bible does not dismiss these experiences, but it places them within clear and careful boundaries.

Holding experience and the Bible together

The Bible acknowledges that God can and does lead His people in specific ways at particular times. At the same time, it consistently resists allowing experience to become the primary guide. Experiences must be tested, not trusted automatically. John issues a sober warning: *"Do not believe every spirit, but test the spirits to see whether they are from God."* (1 John 4:1).

This command assumes that not every impression or inner prompting originates with God. Discernment is required. The Spirit's work never contradicts God's revealed truth.

Paul reinforces this when he urges believers to *"test everything; hold on to what is good."* (1 Thessalonians 5:21). Testing always presupposes criteria and the Bible provides those criteria. Any experience that undermines obedience, humility, love, or truth is not leading believers deeper into God's will, regardless of how compelling it feels. This balanced approach honours the Spirit without elevating subjective experience above the Bible.

The limited role of impressions and promptings

Many believers struggle because they assume that impressions and promptings must play a central role in guidance. The Bible treats such experiences as occasional rather than normative. When they occur, they are usually tied to God's redemptive purposes rather than personal preference.

In the book of Acts, the Spirit occasionally directs believers in specific ways. Yet even there, these moments are selective and purposeful. They do not form a pattern for everyday decision-making. Most of the time, believers act wisely, plan thoughtfully, and adjust as circumstances unfold.

Paul's ministry illustrates this well. At times he is restrained or redirected by the Spirit (Acts 16:6–7). At other times, he makes plans based on wisdom and opportunity. *"After I have been there, I must visit Rome also."* (Acts 19:21). The Bible presents both without tension. The Spirit is at work in both. This prevents believers from assuming that the absence of strong impressions means God is silent or distant. God's guidance is often quiet and ordinary.

Why the Bible warns against chasing signs

A fixation on signs is not encouraged in the Bible. In fact, it is often treated with caution. Jesus warns against a sign-seeking mentality when He says, *"A wicked and adulterous generation asks for a sign."* (Matthew 16:4). The issue is not that God never gives signs, but that seeking them can become a substitute for trust.

Sign-seeking often arises from anxiety rather than faith. Believers want certainty before obedience. The Bible consistently reverses this order. Faith acts on what God has already revealed and trusts Him with what remains unknown.

When believers chase signs, they run the risk of misinterpreting coincidence, emotion, or desire as divine instruction. This does not deepen faith. It destabilises it. The Bible calls believers to anchor themselves in God's promises rather than in fleeting experiences.

The Spirit's guidance through conviction

One of the Spirit's clearest and most reliable forms of guidance is conviction. In John 16:8, Jesus promises that the Spirit will *"prove the world to be in the wrong about sin and righteousness and judgment."* Conviction is moral and relational. It draws believers toward holiness and away from sin.

Conviction is very different from a vague unease or emotional discomfort. It is very specific, rooted in truth, and leads toward repentance and restoration. When believers experience this kind of conviction, they can be confident that the Spirit is at work.

This form of guidance is often overlooked because it does not answer questions about careers or locations. Yet the Bible treats holiness as central to God's will. *"It is God's will that you should be sanctified."* (1 Thessalonians 4:3). The Spirit's work in this area is clear and ongoing. As believers respond to conviction, their sensitivity to God's will deepens. Guidance becomes less about direction and more about faithfulness.

Peace as a companion, not a compass

Another common assumption today is that peace functions as a compass, pointing toward the correct decision. The Bible does speak about peace, but it does not present it as a directional tool.

Paul writes in Colossians 3:15, *"Let the peace of Christ rule in your hearts."* In context, peace governs relationships within the church, not individual decision-making. Peace stabilises the heart. It does not necessarily indicate which option to choose.

Peace can accompany wise decisions, but it can also accompany unwise ones. Likewise, obedience can sometimes be deeply unsettling. Jesus Himself experiences anguish in Gethsemane (Matthew 26:38-39) while submitting perfectly to the Father's will. Peace, therefore, cannot be treated as a reliable guide on its own.

The Bible presents peace as a gift that guards the heart as believers trust God, not as a signal that removes the need for discernment.

Learning to discern without anxiety

When experience is placed in its proper biblical context, discernment becomes calmer and more grounded. Believers are no longer pressured to interpret every feeling or impression. They are free to weigh experiences thoughtfully alongside the Bible, wisdom, and counsel.

Paul urges believers to grow in discernment: *"And this is my prayer: that your love may abound more and more in knowledge and depth of insight, so that you may be able to discern what is best."* (Philippians 1:9-10). Discernment is firmly linked to love, knowledge, and insight. It is cultivated over time.

This growth requires patience. Believers are not expected to master discernment instantly. They learn through practice, reflection, and community. God is patient in this process. He does not abandon His people when they struggle to interpret experiences.

The Spirit's quiet faithfulness

Perhaps the most important truth to grasp is that the Spirit's guidance is usually quiet. It does not draw attention to itself. It works steadily through the Bible, prayer, conscience, and community.

Jesus reassures His disciples, *"But when he, the Spirit of truth, comes, he will guide you into all the truth."* (John 16:13). This guidance unfolds over time. It deepens understanding. It shapes character. It produces faithfulness.

Believers honour the Spirit not by demanding constant direction, but by living attentively and obediently. The Spirit's work becomes evident not in dramatic moments, but in lives marked by wisdom, humility, and trust.

In this way, guidance becomes less about interpreting our experiences and more about living faithfully. The Holy Spirit does not replace wisdom. He forms it. And as believers grow in that wisdom, they find themselves living more confidently and peacefully within the will of God.

As believers learn to recognise the Holy Spirit's guidance through wisdom, conviction, and formation rather than constant instruction, a healthier pattern of dependence begins to emerge. The Spirit is no longer treated as a substitute for responsibility, but as the One who empowers faithful living within it.

Walking by the Spirit in everyday life

The Bible consistently calls believers to *walk* by the Spirit. This language is deliberate. Walking implies rhythm, movement, and ongoing attentiveness. It does not imply constant consultation or dramatic interruption.

Paul writes, *"So I say, walk by the Spirit, and you will not gratify the desires of the flesh."* (Galatians 5:16). The emphasis here is not on guidance for specific choices, but on a way of living shaped by the Spirit. As believers walk by the Spirit, sinful patterns lose their power, and Christlike character takes root.

This way of life does not remove the need for decision-making. It reshapes it. Decisions are made from within a Spirit-shaped life rather than by seeking external direction. God's will is lived out as believers consistently respond to the Spirit's work within them.

Maturity as the goal of guidance

One of the clearest indicators of the Holy Spirit's work is our growing towards maturity. The Bible never presents perpetual dependence on guidance as spiritual maturity. Instead, maturity is marked by discernment, stability, and wisdom.

The writer to the Hebrews contrasts immaturity and maturity by noting that mature believers are those *"who by constant use have trained themselves to distinguish good from evil."* (Hebrews 5:14).

Training implies practice. Discernment grows as believers engage with life under God's Word. This then challenges the assumption that spiritually mature believers always need more guidance. The Bible suggests the opposite. As maturity increases, the need for explicit direction decreases. Believers become increasingly capable of recognising what aligns with God's will. This does not diminish dependence on God. It deepens it. Mature believers depend on God's character and promises rather than on constant instruction.

The Spirit's role in freedom

The Holy Spirit is consistently associated with freedom in the New Testament. Paul declares, *"Now the Lord is the Spirit, and where the Spirit of the Lord is, there is freedom."* (2 Corinthians 3:17). This freedom is not lawlessness. It is freedom from fear, condemnation, and compulsion.

Spirit-led freedom enables believers to act responsibly without anxiety. They are no longer paralysed by the fear of missing God's will. They trust that the Spirit is at work within them, shaping their desires and guiding their steps as they walk in faith.

This freedom also guards against legalism. Believers do not measure faithfulness by rigid rules or external conformity. They measure it by love, obedience, and trust. The Spirit leads believers into lives that reflect the character of Christ rather than mere compliance with expectations.

Discernment in community

The Spirit's guidance is rarely individualistic. The Bible places discernment within the life of the community. Believers are encouraged to listen to one another, test insights together, and grow collectively in wisdom. Paul urges the church, *"Let the word of Christ dwell in you richly... teaching and admonishing one another."* (Colossians 3:16).

The Spirit works through this shared engagement with the Word. Guidance emerges as believers speak truth to one another in love.

Community provides balance. It guards against overconfidence and isolation. It also protects believers from mistaking personal preference for divine guidance. The Spirit often uses the wisdom of others to confirm, challenge, or refine understanding.

When the Spirit leads through circumstances

The Bible does acknowledge that God can use circumstances as part of His guidance. Doors may open or close in ways that shape opportunities. Paul refers to this when he writes, *"A great door for effective work has opened to me."* (1 Corinthians 16:9). Therefore, circumstances can indicate opportunity.

Yet the Bible never treats circumstances as definitive proof of God's will. Open doors may require wisdom. Closed doors may invite perseverance. Circumstances must be interpreted, not simply followed.

The Spirit helps believers interpret circumstances wisely rather than react to them impulsively. Guidance involves discernment, not assumption. God's will cannot be read off events alone.

Confidence without presumption

Walking by the Spirit will therefore produce confidence without presumption. Believers act decisively while remaining humble. They plan without demanding control. They move forward without assuming certainty.

James captures this posture when he writes, *"You ought to say, 'If it is the Lord's will, we will live and do this or that.'"* (James 4:15). This is not hesitation. It is humility. Plans are made in awareness of God's sovereignty.

This balance protects believers from two extremes. It guards against passivity that waits endlessly for direction, and against arrogance that ignores God altogether. The Spirit leads believers into lives marked by trustful action.

The Spirit's work over a lifetime

Perhaps the most important truth about the Spirit's guidance is that it unfolds over a lifetime. The Spirit's goal is not to produce perfect decisions, but faithful people. Guidance is not a series of moments. It is a long process of formation.

Paul expresses this lifelong confidence when he writes, *"We all... are being transformed into his image with ever-increasing glory, which comes from the Lord, who is the Spirit."* (2 Corinthians 3:18). Transformation is ongoing. God's will is being worked out continuously as believers are shaped into the image of Christ.

This perspective brings peace. Believers do not need to master guidance techniques. They need to remain responsive to the Spirit's work. God is patient. He is faithful. He continues to lead His people as they walk with Him.

Living responsively before God

In the end, the Spirit's guidance calls believers into a responsive life. They listen to God's Word, attend to the Spirit's work, seek wisdom, and act faithfully. They trust God with outcomes they cannot control.

This way of life honours both God's sovereignty and human responsibility. It reflects the Bible's vision of mature faith. Believers are not driven by fear or obsessed with certainty. They are grounded in trust.

As believers walk by the Spirit in this way, God's will no longer feels distant or confusing. It becomes the lived reality of a life shaped by God's presence, guided by His truth, and sustained by His grace.

8. FREEDOM AND THE DECISIONS WE MAKE

By this point in our study, a consistent biblical pattern has emerged. God's will is not hidden behind a maze of decisions, nor is it revealed through constant instruction.

It is lived out each day through faith, wisdom, and obedience within a secure relationship with God. This raises a very practical question: how should believers actually make decisions day by day in light of this understanding?

For many Christians, decision-making remains the most anxious part of their faith. Even after rejecting blueprint thinking in theory, old habits persist in practice. The Bible offers a calmer, sturdier approach, one that honours both God's sovereignty and genuine human responsibility.

Freedom that is real and responsible

The Bible speaks unapologetically about Christian freedom. This freedom is not marginal or conditional. It flows directly from the gospel. Paul declares, *"It is for freedom that Christ has set us free."* (Galatians 5:1). Freedom is not a reward for spiritual maturity. It is part of what Christ has already accomplished.

Yet this freedom is never presented as reckless or self-serving. The Bible consistently holds freedom and responsibility together. Paul writes, *"You were called to be free. But do not use your freedom to indulge the flesh; rather, serve one another humbly in love."* (Galatians 5:13). Freedom is very real, but it is shaped by love, humility, and obedience.

This balance is crucial for decision-making. Believers are not constrained by fear, nor are they left without moral boundaries. They are free to choose among many legitimate options, while remaining accountable to God for how those choices reflect His character.

Understanding this frees believers from the illusion that only one decision could ever honour God. The Bible simply does not support that idea.

Many decisions fall within the realm of wisdom rather than obedience. God's will is not threatened by choice. It is expressed through it.

Wisdom as the ordinary means of guidance

When the Bible speaks about how believers should make decisions, it overwhelmingly emphasises wisdom. Wisdom is not mysterious or rare. It is God's ordinary provision for navigating a complex world.

James encourages believers to ask God for wisdom with confidence: *"If any of you lacks wisdom, you should ask God, who gives generously to all without finding fault."* (James 1:5). Notice what is promised. Wisdom is given. Certainty is not. God equips His people to think well, not to see the future.

The book of Proverbs reinforces this pattern again and again. Wisdom is portrayed as something learned over time, through instruction, experience, and reflection. *"The plans of the diligent lead surely to abundance."* (Proverbs 21:5). Planning, diligence, and foresight are affirmed as wise and godly.

This means believers should not apologise for thinking carefully, weighing options, or considering consequences. These are not signs of weak faith. They are expressions of it. Wisdom honours God by taking responsibility seriously.

Making decisions without spiritual paralysis

One of the most damaging effects of misunderstanding God's will is paralysis. Believers hesitate, delay, and overanalyse, fearing that movement without certainty is disobedience. the Bible does not encourage this posture.

Ecclesiastes 11:4 offers an observation: *"Whoever watches the wind will not plant; whoever looks at the clouds will not reap."* Waiting for perfect conditions leads to inaction. Life requires movement in the presence of uncertainty. The New Testament reflects this same realism. Paul plans, travels, adapts, and changes course as needed. He does not wait for guaranteed outcomes. He acts in faith, trusting God with the results.

"I planted the seed, Apollos watered it, but God has been making it grow." (1 Corinthians 3:6). Human responsibility and divine sovereignty operate together. Believers honour God not by avoiding decisions, but by making them prayerfully and responsibly. Faith does not eliminate risk. It entrusts risk to God.

Evaluating decisions in a Biblical way

The Bible provides clear criteria for evaluating decisions, even when it does not specify outcomes. Paul offers a helpful framework when he asks, *"'I have the right to do anything,' you say – but not everything is beneficial."* (1 Corinthians 6:12). Not every permissible choice is wise.

Questions of benefit, fruitfulness, and impact matter. Does a decision promote love? Does it encourage faithfulness? Does it build others up? These are deeply biblical questions. They shift attention away from fear and toward responsibility.

In Romans 14:22, Paul also urges all believers to consider our conscience: *"Blessed is the one who does not condemn himself by what he approves."* A clear conscience matters. Decisions should be made honestly, without self-deception or pressure. None of this requires special revelation. It requires attentiveness to the Bible, awareness of one's own heart, and willingness to act in faith.

A calm confidence in God's care

Perhaps the greatest change that will come from a more biblical understanding of decision-making is emotional. Anxiety gives way to confidence, not confidence in oneself, but confidence in God's care.

Proverbs offers a steady promise: *"Trust in the Lord with all your heart and lean not on your own understanding; in all your ways submit to him, and he will make your paths straight."* (Proverbs 3:5–6). This does not mean God removes all uncertainty. It means He faithfully directs those who trust Him as they walk forward. Believers are not navigating life alone. God is actively at work, guiding, correcting, and sustaining them. Decisions are made within His care, not outside it.

As freedom and wisdom take their proper place, decision-making becomes less fearful and more faithful. God's will is not something fragile that must be protected from mistakes. It is the gracious purpose of a faithful God who walks with His people as they choose, act, learn, and grow before Him.

If freedom and wisdom form the biblical framework for decision-making, then the way believers *approach* decisions matters just as much as the decisions themselves. The Bible does not call God's people to reckless independence or anxious dependence, but to a thoughtful, prayerful engagement with life that reflects trust in God's character.

Prayer that shapes perspective

Prayer plays a vital role in decision-making, but not in the way it is often assumed. The Bible does not present prayer as a means of extracting answers from God, as though the right question will produce exactly the right instruction. Instead, prayer reshapes perspective.

Paul exhorts believers, *"Do not be anxious about anything, but in every situation, by prayer and petition, with thanksgiving, present your requests to God."* (Philippians 4:6). The result he describes is not immediate clarity, but peace: *"And the peace of God... will guard your hearts and your minds in Christ Jesus."* (Philippians 4:7). Prayer calms the heart and steadies the mind. It does not remove the responsibility to decide.

In prayer, believers bring their desires, fears, and uncertainties before God. They honestly acknowledge dependence without surrendering responsibility. Prayer reminds them that God is present and faithful, even when choices remain complex. This posture guards against panic-driven decisions and fear-based delay.

Weighing consequences without fear

Therefore, the Bible consistently affirms the value of considering consequences. Wisdom involves foresight. *"The prudent see danger and take refuge, but the simple keep going and pay the penalty"* (Proverbs 22:3).

Prudence is not a lack of faith. It is an expression of it. Believers are encouraged to think realistically about outcomes. Jesus Himself uses this principle when He speaks about counting the cost (Luke 14:28). He does not condemn calculation. Rather, He condemns shallow commitment. Thoughtfulness honours God by recognising that choices affect others and shape the future.

At the same time, the Bible clearly guards against fear-driven calculation. Worry is not wisdom. *"Who of you by worrying can add a single hour to your life?"* (Matthew 6:27). Considering the consequences should lead to responsibility, not paralysis. Believers weigh options honestly, then entrust outcomes to God.

The place of desire and inclination

Desire is often treated with suspicion in discussions about God's will. While the Bible warns against sinful desires, it does not portray desire itself as unreliable or unspiritual. God works within the desires of redeemed people.

The psalmist declares, *"Take delight in the Lord, and he will give you the desires of your heart."* (Psalm 37:4). As believers delight in God, their desires are reshaped. Inclinations begin to reflect God's values rather than compete with them.

Paul reinforces this truth in Philippians 2:13, *"For it is God who works in you to will and to act according to his good purpose."* God is at work not only in actions, but in intentions. This means believers need not distrust every desire automatically. Instead, they test desires in the light of the Bible, wisdom, and love.

When desires align with God's revealed will and are pursued with humility, they can legitimately inform decisions. God's guidance is not opposed to desire. It transforms it.

Acting decisively with humility

A biblical approach to decision-making leads not to endless analysis, but to decisive action marked by humility. The Bible encourages believers to move forward while holding their plans loosely. James offers this balanced perspective: *"You ought to say, 'If it is the Lord's will, we will live and do this or that.'"* (James 4:15).

This is not hesitation. It is acknowledgement. Believers plan, decide, and act, while recognising that God remains sovereign over outcomes. Humility does not require uncertainty. It requires trust. Believers act decisively because inaction is also a choice, often a costly one. They move forward prayerfully, ready to learn, adjust, and grow as life unfolds.

This posture frees believers from the burden of needing guarantees. They do not need to know how everything will turn out. They need to trust the God who walks with them.

Confidence rooted in God's faithfulness

Ultimately, confidence in decision-making does not come from perfect discernment. It comes from having confidence in God's faithfulness. The Bible repeatedly affirms that God is committed to His people over the long course of their lives.

The psalmist writes, *"Commit your way to the Lord; trust in him and he will do this."* (Psalm 37:5). The promise is not that God will reveal every detail, but that He will be faithful as believers entrust their lives to Him.

As believers grow in this confidence, decision-making becomes steadier and less anxious. They are free to think, choose, and act responsibly, trusting that God is at work in them and through them.

Freedom, wisdom, prayer, and trust converge here. God's will is not something fragile that must be discovered with precision. It is the gracious context in which believers live faithfully, making real decisions with calm confidence in the God who is faithful in every season of life.

When freedom and wisdom are embraced together, decision-making begins to look less like a spiritual ordeal and more like an expression of faithful living.

The Bible does not promise that decisions will always be easy or that outcomes will always be favourable. What it does promise is that God remains faithful as His people live responsibly before Him.

Learning to live with the consequences of choice

One of the realities the Bible never avoids is that choices have consequences. This is not presented as a threat, but as part of living in a real world under God's moral order. As Paul wrote, *"Do not be deceived: God cannot be mocked. A man reaps what he sows."* (Galatians 6:7). This principle applies broadly to life, not merely to moments of moral failure.

For believers, this truth is not meant to produce fear, but maturity. Decisions matter because life matters. The Bible assumes that faithful people will experience both positive and painful consequences, sometimes simultaneously, and yet these consequences do not define whether a decision was made within God's will.

Paul's life illustrates this clearly. His obedience leads to hardship, imprisonment, and suffering, yet he does not interpret these outcomes as evidence of error. He understands them as part of faithful service. *"I consider my life worth nothing to me; my only aim is to finish the race and complete the task the Lord Jesus has given me."* (Acts 20:24).

Believers are called to own their choices without being crushed by them. God's grace meets them not only in success, but also in difficulty.

God's grace in imperfect decisions

A biblical approach to decision-making must make room for imperfection. The Bible never suggests that believers will choose flawlessly. It consistently points instead to God's grace as the sustaining reality of the Christian life.

In 2 Corinthians 12:9, Paul captures this posture when he writes, *"My grace is sufficient for you, for my power is made perfect in weakness."* God's grace does not wait until believers get everything right. It meets them in weakness, uncertainty, and limitation. This truth protects believers from despair when decisions do not lead where they hoped. God is not absent from imperfect choices. He remains present, working redemptively within them.

This does not excuse irresponsibility, but it relieves crushing guilt. The Bible invites believers to learn rather than to retreat. Growth often comes through reflection on past decisions, guided by God's Word and shaped by humility.

Adjusting course without shame

Another mark of wise decision-making is the willingness to adjust course. The Bible does not equate changing direction with failure. It often portrays it as wisdom.

Paul himself adjusts his plans repeatedly in response to circumstances, counsel, and opportunity. He holds his intentions firmly, yet humbly. This flexibility reflects trust in God rather than attachment to outcomes.

Proverbs affirms this posture: *"In their hearts humans plan their course, but the Lord establishes their steps."* (Proverbs 16:9). Planning and adjustment are not opposites. They work together. Believers plan responsibly, then remain open to God's ongoing work.

This openness frees believers from defensiveness. They do not need to justify every past decision. They can learn, change, and move forward without shame, trusting that God continues to guide them.

Faithfulness over a lifetime

The Bible consistently evaluates faithfulness over the course of a life rather than in isolated moments. God's will is not revealed in a single decision, but in the overall direction of a person's walk with Him.

Paul reflects this long-term perspective in 2 Timothy 4:7, *"I have fought the good fight, I have finished the race, I have kept the faith."* Faithfulness is measured in perseverance, not perfection.

This perspective reshapes how believers view their decisions. Individual choices matter, but they are not ultimate. What matters most is the ongoing posture of trust, obedience, and humility before God.

As believers walk with God over time, their lives begin to display coherence. Patterns of faithfulness emerge. Wisdom deepens. Confidence grows. God's will is not something they must continually locate. It is something that shapes them as they live.

Freedom that leads to peace

When believers accept responsibility without fear, decision-making becomes a source of peace rather than anxiety. This peace is not rooted in certainty about outcomes, but in trust in God's care.

Jesus reassures His disciples, *"Peace I leave with you; my peace I give you... Do not let your hearts be troubled and do not be afraid."* (John 14:27). This peace coexists with uncertainty. It steadies the heart even when the future is unclear.

Paul encourages believers to allow this peace to guard their hearts as they trust God (Philippians 4:7). Peace does not remove decisions. It sustains believers as they make them.

A confident way forward

As this chapter draws together, a clear biblical pattern stands out. God has not left His people without guidance. He has given them freedom shaped by wisdom, the Bible, prayer, and community. He has not asked them to eliminate uncertainty. He has asked them to trust Him within it.

Believers are free to decide, act, and grow. They are free to learn from experience and to adjust course when needed. They are free from the fear that one wrong choice will undo God's purposes.

God's will is not a fragile plan dependent on perfect decisions. It is the faithful purpose of a gracious God who walks with His people through every season of life. As believers live within that will, they discover that freedom and wisdom are not obstacles to faith. They are gifts that enable them to live fully, responsibly, and peacefully before God.

9. WHEN GUIDANCE FEELS SILENT

For many believers, one of the most unsettling experiences in the Christian life is the sense that God is silent. They pray, read the Bible, seek counsel, and yet still feel uncertain about what to do. In a culture that all too often equates guidance with clarity and immediacy, silence is easily interpreted as absence, disapproval, or failure. The Bible, however, offers a very different framework for understanding seasons when guidance feels quiet. Rather than treating silence as a problem to be solved, the Bible invites believers to see it as a normal and often necessary part of faithful living.

Silence does not mean God is absent

One of the most damaging assumptions believers make is that silence equals abandonment. When clarity does not come, they assume God has withdrawn or is withholding guidance. The Bible consistently rejects this conclusion.

In Psalm 13:1, the psalmist gives voice to the experience of divine silence while refusing to equate it with absence: *"How long, Lord? Will you forget me forever? How long will you hide your face from me?"* The question itself assumes relationship. The psalmist continues to pray because he knows God is still there, even when He feels distant.

God's promises confirm this reality. *"Never will I leave you; never will I forsake you."* (Hebrews 13:5). This deep assurance is not conditional on clarity or emotional awareness. God's presence is a fact, not something believers must infer from circumstances. When guidance feels silent, the Bible calls believers to trust what God has already revealed about His faithfulness. Silence does not negate God's commitment. It often tests trust in it.

Why the Bible normalises waiting

Waiting is woven deeply into the biblical story. Far from being a sign of weak faith, waiting is often portrayed as an essential context for its growth. God's people regularly experience periods where direction is not immediately clear.

Isaiah captures this posture when he writes, *"Those who hope in the Lord will renew their strength."* (Isaiah 40:31). Hope here is not passive resignation. It is active trust exercised over time. Waiting stretches faith by requiring believers to live without immediate resolution.

The psalms repeatedly return to this theme. *"I wait for the Lord, my whole being waits, and in his word I put my hope."* (Psalm 130:5). Notice where hope is anchored. Not in new information, but in God's word. Waiting does not suspend obedience. It deepens reliance on what God has already said.

The Bible never presents waiting as wasted time. It is formative time. God uses waiting to reshape priorities, expose motives, and strengthen dependence on Him.

The difference between silence and sufficiency

Often what believers experience as silence is not the absence of guidance, but the sufficiency of what God has already provided. The Bible repeatedly affirms that God has given His people everything they need for faithful living.

Peter writes, *"His divine power has given us everything we need for a godly life."* (2 Peter 1:3). If this is true, then God is not withholding essential guidance. He is inviting believers to live out what they already know.

In many cases, believers are asking God to clarify decisions that the Bible has already framed. Questions about integrity, love, faithfulness, and obedience are not unanswered. God's will in these areas is clear. Silence often occurs not because God has nothing to say, but because He has already spoken.

This reframes how silence is understood. It is not neglect. It is trust. God entrusts His people with responsibility shaped by His Word and sustained by His presence.

Acting faithfully when clarity does not come

The Bible does not instruct believers to suspend all action until clarity arrives. On the contrary, in fact, it consistently encourages faithful action grounded in trust.

Paul told us, *"We live by faith, not by sight."* (2 Corinthians 5:7). Faith moves forward without complete visibility. Ecclesiastes offers a clear image: *"Sow your seed in the morning, and at evening let your hands not be idle, for you do not know which will succeed."* (Ecclesiastes 11:6). Uncertainty does not excuse our inaction. It calls for diligence and trust.

This does not mean rushing decisions or ignoring wisdom. It means refusing to equate uncertainty with disobedience. Believers are free to act responsibly, trusting that God is present and at work even when guidance feels quiet.

Learning to trust God's character

Ultimately, seasons of silence shift the focus from guidance to character. When believers cannot rely on clarity, they must rely on who God is. The Bible consistently directs attention here.

The psalmist declares, *"The Lord is gracious and righteous; our God is full of compassion."* (Psalm 116:5). Trust in God's character sustains faith when answers are delayed. God's goodness does not fluctuate with circumstances.

Silence exposes what believers trust most. If faith depends on constant reassurance, silence will feel unbearable. If faith rests on God's revealed character, silence becomes survivable, even strengthening.

As believers learn to trust God in silence, their faith matures. They discover that guidance is not always a voice giving directions. Often it is the quiet assurance that God is faithful, present, and trustworthy as they continue to walk before Him. In this way, silence does not undermine God's will. It deepens reliance on the God whose will is already at work, even when the path ahead is not yet clear.

When God's guidance feels silent, the greatest danger is not uncertainty itself, but how believers interpret it. Silence has a way of amplifying fears and assumptions, often leading people to conclusions the Bible does not support. Understanding what silence is *not* - is just as important as understanding what it is.

Silence is not punishment or disapproval

One of the most common assumptions believers make is that silence signals God's displeasure. They search their lives for hidden sin, unresolved failure, or those missed opportunities, convinced that God has withdrawn His guidance as a form of correction. The Bible does not lead us to this conclusion.

The challenging book of Job confronts this assumption directly. Job experiences profound silence from God in the midst of suffering, yet the Bible is clear that his hardship is not the result of divine disapproval. In fact, God affirms Job's integrity even while remaining silent for long stretches (Job 1:8). Silence, in this case, is not judgment. It is mystery.

David expresses a similar struggle: *"My God, my God, why have you forsaken me?"* (Psalm 22:1). This cry is not evidence of abandonment, but of honest faith under pressure. The psalm moves from anguish to trust, reminding readers that silence does not erase relationship.

Believers must be careful not to interpret silence as rejection. God's love and acceptance are grounded in Christ, not in the immediacy of felt guidance. *"God demonstrates his own love for us in this: While we were still sinners, Christ died for us."* (Romans 5:8). That love is not withdrawn when answers are delayed.

When silence tests motives

Silence often exposes why believers seek guidance in the first place. At times, the desire for guidance is less about obedience and more about reassurance. Believers may want certainty not to honour God, but to avoid risk, discomfort, or responsibility.

The Bible regularly confronts this tendency. Jesus rebukes those who demand signs while ignoring what God may have already revealed (Matthew 12:39). The problem here is not a lack of information, but a reluctance to trust. When God remains silent, He may be inviting believers to examine their motives. Are they seeking guidance to obey, or to be protected from uncertainty? Silence removes the safety net of certainty and reveals what truly drives the heart.

This testing is not cruel. It is formative. God uses silence to purify faith, shifting it from reliance on answers to reliance on Him.

God's pattern of speaking and then waiting

A striking pattern throughout the Bible is that God often speaks clearly and then allows long periods of apparent silence. Abraham receives a promise from God, then waits decades for its fulfilment. Israel receives God's law, then lives under it through centuries without new revelation. The early church receives Christ's teaching, then spreads the gospel guided by the Bible and wisdom.

This pattern suggests that silence is not a failure of guidance, but a feature of it. God does not repeat Himself endlessly. He expects His people to live faithfully in light of what He has already said. Jesus reflects this pattern when He says, *"Why do you call me, 'Lord, Lord,' and do not do what I say?"* (Luke 6:46). Obedience does not require fresh instruction. It requires faithfulness to what has already been revealed.

When believers ask God to speak again when He has already spoken clearly, silence may be an invitation to act rather than to wait.

Learning to live without immediate answers

The Bible repeatedly affirms that faith involves living without immediate answers. Hebrews 11:1 describes faith as *"confidence in what we hope for and assurance about what we do not see."* Faith does not eliminate unanswered questions. It sustains trust in their presence.

So, the lives of faithful believers will be marked by incomplete understanding. They act on God's promises without knowing how those promises will unfold. Abraham sets out *"even though he did not know where he was going."* (Hebrews 11:8). Faith moves forward without full explanation.

Silence forces believers into this posture. It prevents faith from collapsing into control. When answers are withheld, trust must deepen or be abandoned. The Bible consistently calls believers to deepen trust.

Obedience in the absence of clarity

One of the clearest biblical responses to silence is obedience in the present. God's will is rarely unclear in matters of character, love, and faithfulness. Silence about the future does not excuse disobedience in the present.

Jesus addresses this directly when He asks, *"Whoever can be trusted with very little can also be trusted with much."* (Luke 16:10). Faithfulness in small, clear responsibilities prepares believers for larger ones. Silence often redirects attention to what is already known and neglected.

Paul echoes this emphasis in 1 Thessalonians 4:11, *"Make it your ambition to lead a quiet life… and to work with your hands."* Ordinary obedience matters deeply to God. It does not require special guidance. It requires faithfulness. When believers remain obedient in silence, they discover that silence does not stall spiritual growth. It often accelerates it.

Silence as an invitation to deeper trust

Ultimately, silence presses believers toward a deeper trust in God's character. When guidance is not immediate, faith must rest on who God is rather than on what He says next.

Isaiah captures this trust when he writes, *"Here is my servant, whom I uphold, my chosen one in whom I delight."* (Isaiah 42:1). God's delight in His servant is not conditional on constant instruction. It is rooted in relationship.

For believers, this trust is grounded in Christ. God has spoken finally and decisively in His Son. Silence does not contradict that revelation. It rests upon it.

As believers learn to trust God in silence, they begin to recognise that silence itself can be a form of guidance. It directs them away from dependence on answers and toward dependence on God. In that place, faith matures, confidence deepens, and obedience becomes steadier, even when the way forward remains unclear. As believers learn to live faithfully through seasons when guidance feels silent, something profound takes place.

Silence no longer appears as an obstacle to God's will, but as a context in which trust, maturity, and obedience are deepened. What once felt unsettling becomes formative.

Silence and the maturing of our faith

The Bible consistently presents maturity as the ability to trust God without constant reassurance. This does not diminish the importance of prayer or the Bible. It just reshapes their role. Faith moves from dependence on clarity to a deep confidence in God's character.

James writes, *"Consider it pure joy... whenever you face trials of many kinds, because you know that the testing of your faith produces perseverance."* (James 1:2–3). Silence often functions as a form of testing, not to expose failure, but to produce endurance. God is less interested in immediate certainty than in lasting faithfulness. As perseverance grows, believers become less reactive and more grounded. They learn that faith does not require constant confirmation. It requires trust sustained over time.

When silence guards against idolatry

One of the subtler dangers in the pursuit of guidance is the temptation to make certainty an idol. Believers may come to trust clarity more than God Himself. Silence disrupts this pattern.

The Bible repeatedly warns against misplaced trust. *"Some trust in chariots and some in horses, but we trust in the name of the Lord our God."* (Psalm 20:7). In a modern context, clarity can function as a chariot. When God withholds it, He may be protecting believers from trusting the wrong thing.

Silence strips away false securities. It reveals whether faith rests on God or on the comfort of knowing what comes next. This exposure is uncomfortable, but it is merciful. God's will is not served by misplaced trust.

The quiet work God is still doing

Silence should never be confused with inactivity. The Bible affirms that God is always at work, even when His voice is not heard in the ways believers expect.

Jesus reassures His followers, *"My Father is always at his work to this very day, and I too am working."* (John 5:17). God's work continues regardless of human perception. Silence often conceals activity rather than indicating its absence.

Paul echoes this confidence: *"The one who calls you is faithful, and he will do it."* (1 Thessalonians 5:24). God's faithfulness does not depend on the immediacy of guidance. His purposes advance steadily, even when unseen. Believers may even recognise later that God was shaping them more deeply in silence than in seasons of clarity. Silence slows them down, quiets distractions, and deepens dependence.

Faithful living without immediate direction

The Bible consistently calls believers to live faithfully even when the future remains unclear. This kind of faith honours God by trusting Him with what cannot yet be known.

The psalmist models this trust when he writes, *"My times are in your hands."* (Psalm 31:15). This statement does not follow clarity. It follows surrender. Faith entrusts the future to God without demanding a timetable. This posture will enable believers to continue loving, serving, and obeying in the present.

Silence does not suspend faithfulness. It refines it. God's will is lived out in daily obedience, not postponed until answers arrive.

How silence shapes prayer

Prayer itself is transformed in silence. Instead of focusing on requests for direction, prayer becomes a place of surrender, honesty, and trust.

Jesus' prayer in Gethsemane embodies this posture. *"Yet not as I will, but as you will."* (Matthew 26:39). This prayer does not seek clarity. It submits to God's will in the absence of escape. It reflects trust at the deepest level.

Believers learn in silence that prayer is not only about asking. It is also about resting in God's presence. Silence creates space for listening, not necessarily for words, but for trust to grow.

Living confidently when God is quiet

As silence loses its power to unsettle, believers begin to live more confidently. They are no longer paralysed by the absence of direction. They act responsibly, trust God with outcomes, and remain attentive to His Word.

Proverbs offers a steady promise: *"In all your ways submit to him, and he will make your paths straight."* (Proverbs 3:6). This does not require constant communication. It requires consistent trust.

Believers discover that God's will does not disappear in silence. It remains active, shaping their lives from within. Silence does not interrupt God's purposes. It often strengthens them.

From anxiety to assurance

As this chapter draws together, the transformation becomes clear. Anxiety gives way to assurance, not because uncertainty is resolved, but because trust has deepened. Believers no longer interpret silence as failure or abandonment. They recognise it as part of God's wise and faithful care.

God's will is not fragile. It does not depend on constant direction. It is rooted in God's unchanging character and faithful presence. As believers learn to live through silence, they find that God is as trustworthy in quiet seasons as in clear ones.

Silence, then, becomes not a void to be feared, but a space in which faith matures, hope strengthens, and obedience becomes steadier. God remains at work, guiding His people not always by words, but by shaping hearts that trust Him, even when the way forward is not yet revealed.

10. WHEN CIRCUMSTANCES CHANGE AND PLANS UNRAVEL

One of the moments when questions about God's will return with renewed force is when carefully made plans begin to unravel.

Believers may have acted prayerfully, sought wisdom, and moved forward in good faith, only to find doors closing, circumstances shifting, or outcomes diverging sharply from expectations. In those moments, the temptation is strong to revisit every decision and ask whether God's will was somehow missed.

The Bible speaks very directly into this experience. It neither romanticises disrupted plans nor treats them as spiritual failure. Instead, it provides a framework for understanding change, disappointment, and redirection within the faithful purposes of God.

The Bible assumes plans will change

The Bible never assumes that human plans will unfold exactly as intended. In fact, the Bible repeatedly normalises change and disruption.

Proverbs states this plainly: *"In their hearts humans plan their course, but the Lord establishes their steps."* (Proverbs 16:9). Planning is affirmed, not criticised. Yet final outcomes remain in God's hands.

This balance appears throughout the Bible. James cautions believers against presumption, not planning itself: *"You do not even know what will happen tomorrow... You ought to say, 'If it is the Lord's will, we will live and do this or that.'"* (James 4:14–15). The issue is not that plans are made, but that they are held humbly.

The Bible assumes believers will plan responsibly while remaining open to change. When plans unravel, this does not automatically signal error. It often reflects the normal interaction between human responsibility and divine sovereignty.

God's will is not identical to our plans

A crucial distinction the Bible makes is that God's will is not identical to human planning, even faithful planning. Believers may plan wisely and prayerfully, yet still experience outcomes they did not foresee.

Isaiah records God's own words on this point: *"'My thoughts are not your thoughts, neither are your ways my ways,' declares the Lord."* (Isaiah 55:8). This is not a rebuke of human planning. It is a reminder of perspective. God sees more, knows more, and works more broadly than believers can.

This truth protects believers from two harmful conclusions. It prevents them from assuming that disrupted plans mean God's will has failed, and it prevents them from assuming their plans fully capture God's intentions. God's will encompasses human plans without being limited by them.

When circumstances change, the Bible invites believers to trust that God remains purposeful, even when His purposes differ from their expectations.

Biblical examples of redirected lives

The Bible is filled with examples of faithful people whose plans were redirected. Joseph's early dreams did not include betrayal, slavery, or imprisonment, yet God worked through those very disruptions to bring about His purposes. Joseph later recognises this when he says, *"You intended to harm me, but God intended it for good."* (Genesis 50:20).

Paul's ministry also reflects this pattern. He often planned carefully, only to find his course altered by circumstances, opposition, or limitation. At times he describes these changes as the Lord closing doors; at other times, he simply adapts and continues. Nowhere does he treat change as evidence that God's will was missed.

Instead, Paul expresses confidence that God is at work through both intention and interruption. *"And we know that in all things God works for the good of those who love him."* (Romans 8:28).

This promise does not apply only to successful plans. It applies to disrupted ones as well.

When disappointment feels personal

When plans unravel, disappointment often feels deeply personal. Believers may grieve lost opportunities, wasted effort, or hopes that no longer seem attainable. The Bible does not dismiss this grief. It gives voice to it.

The psalms repeatedly express honest lament. For example, in Psalm 10:1 we read, *"Why, Lord, do you stand far off? Why do you hide yourself in times of trouble?"* These questions are not signs of unbelief. They are expressions of trust that bring pain honestly before God.

The Bible allows believers to grieve without concluding that God has abandoned them. Disappointment does not mean God's will has ceased to operate. It often means God's work is taking a different shape than expected.

Holding faith when the path changes

When circumstances shift, the Bible calls believers not to retreat into self-blame or despair, but to reaffirm trust in God's faithfulness. *"The Lord will fulfil his purpose for me; your love, Lord, endures forever."* (Psalm 138:8). God's purposes are not fragile. They are not undone by change.

Faith in these moments does not require forced optimism. It requires steady trust. Believers are invited to continue walking faithfully, even when the road ahead looks different from what they planned.

Plans may unravel. Paths may change. Yet God's will remains active, shaping lives not only through what succeeds, but also through what is interrupted. Understanding this prepares believers to face change without fear, trusting that God is at work even when plans fall apart.

When plans begin to unravel, believers often feel an intense pressure to interpret events correctly. Every closed door, delay, or unexpected turn can become loaded with meaning.

The Bible encourages a calmer, more grounded response, one that resists over-interpretation while remaining attentive to God's ongoing work.

Closed doors and open doors in the Bible

Christians often speak about "open" and "closed" doors as shorthand for God's guidance. The Bible does use this language, but it does so carefully and sparingly. When Paul writes, *"A great door for effective work has opened to me."* (1 Corinthians 16:9), he is describing opportunity, not certainty. Even with an open door, opposition remains.

Likewise, the Bible records times when Paul is hindered or redirected. *"Paul and his companions travelled throughout the region… having been kept by the Holy Spirit from preaching the word in the province of Asia."* (Acts 16:6). Yet even here, the redirection is tied to the advance of the gospel, not to Paul's personal preferences or comfort. The key point is that the Bible never treats doors as infallible indicators of God's will. Open doors still require wisdom. Closed doors do not automatically signal some kind of failure. Circumstances inform discernment, but they do not replace it.

When believers read too much into circumstances, they risk turning events into messages God never intended to send. The Bible calls for humility in interpretation, not certainty drawn from change alone.

The temptation to rewrite the past

When plans fall apart, many believers instinctively look backward. They replay decisions, searching for the moment they "got it wrong." While reflection can be healthy, the Bible warns against a fixation on regret.

Paul offers a clear example of forward-focused faith: *"Forgetting what is behind and straining toward what is ahead, I press on."* (Philippians 3:13–14). This does not mean denying the past. It means refusing to be defined by it. The Bible never encourages believers to obsess over missed opportunities or alternate outcomes. God's redemptive work is not limited to ideal choices.

He continues to work within the reality that exists, not the one believers wish had unfolded. Looking backward with self-condemnation rarely produces wisdom. It more often produces paralysis. The Bible redirects attention toward faithful living in the present, trusting God with both past and future.

God's purposes are not dependent on stability

Another assumption exposed when plans unravel is the belief that God's will requires stable circumstances. The Bible consistently undermines this idea. God often works most powerfully amid instability, disruption, and uncertainty.

Israel's journey through the wilderness is a striking example. Their route is indirect, uncomfortable, and unpredictable, yet the Bible repeatedly affirms that God is leading them. *"The Lord went ahead of them in a pillar of cloud... and in a pillar of fire by night."* (Exodus 13:21). Here we see that movement, and not permanence, characterises their journey.

The New Testament echoes this theme. Believers are described as pilgrims and strangers (1 Peter 2:11), people whose lives are not marked by settled certainty. God's will unfolds through movement, adaptation, and trust, not through uninterrupted stability. When circumstances change, believers are not stepping outside God's will. They are often experiencing one of its normal rhythms.

Responding faithfully when control is lost

Few things expose the limits of human control like disrupted plans. The Bible invites believers to respond to this loss not with anxiety, but with renewed trust. *"Cast all your anxiety on him because he cares for you."* (1 Peter 5:7). Anxiety thrives where control is clung to. Trust grows where control is surrendered.

Jesus addresses this tendency directly in Matthew 6:19–21, when He warns against storing up security in earthly plans and outcomes. Life cannot be secured by careful planning alone. Faith is required precisely because outcomes remain uncertain. Faithful response does not mean passivity.

Believers continue to act, adapt, and make wise decisions. What changes is the posture of the heart. Control is replaced by trust. Fear is replaced by confidence in God's care.

Learning to discern without panic

When plans unravel, discernment must slow down rather than speed up. Panic-driven interpretation often leads to poor conclusions. The Bible encourages patience and steadiness in uncertain seasons.

The psalmist offers a simple but profound counsel: *"Be still before the Lord and wait patiently for him."* (Psalm 37:7). Stillness does not mean inactivity. It means resisting the urge to force meaning or rush conclusions.

As believers learn to respond calmly to change, they become better equipped to recognise what God is doing over time rather than in isolated moments. Discernment grows not through urgency, but through attentiveness.

Circumstances will continue to change. Plans will continue to unravel. The Bible does not deny this reality. It offers something better: confidence that God's will is not threatened by change, and that faithful living remains possible even when control is lost and the future feels uncertain.

As believers learn to live with changing circumstances, a deeper understanding of God's will begins to take shape. Disrupted plans no longer feel like detours away from God's purposes, but as part of the way those purposes unfold. The Bible consistently affirms that God is at work not only through intention, but through interruption.

God's will at work through change

One of the most stabilising truths the Bible offers is that God's will operates through change rather than in spite of it. God's purposes are not confined to predictable paths. They unfold dynamically within a broken and shifting world. Paul reflects this confidence when he writes, *"We know that in all things God works for the good of those who love him."* (Romans 8:28).

This promise is not limited to circumstances that align neatly with plans. It explicitly includes disruption, disappointment, and loss. God's work is comprehensive.

This does not mean that every change is good in itself. The Bible does not minimise pain or loss. It means that God is able to work redemptively through all of it. His will is not suspended when plans unravel. It is actively shaping lives within the change.

Trusting God beyond outcomes

When plans fall apart, believers often evaluate their faithfulness by outcomes. If things go well, they assume God's will has been followed. If things go poorly, they assume something has gone wrong. The Bible consistently resists this outcome-based assessment.

Jesus' own life offers the clearest example. His obedience leads not to visible success, but to rejection, suffering, and crucifixion. Yet the Bible presents His life as the perfect fulfilment of God's will. *"I have brought you glory on earth by finishing the work you gave me to do."* (John 17:4). Faithfulness is not measured by immediate success.

This perspective frees believers from the need to justify their decisions based on results. God's will is honoured through trust and obedience, not through control of outcomes.

Responding to change with faithful action

The Bible consistently calls believers to respond to change with continued faithfulness. When circumstances shift, obedience does not pause. It adapts. Paul's ministry clearly illustrates this adaptability. When imprisoned, he does not abandon his calling. He writes letters, encourages churches, and proclaims Christ to those around him.

"What has happened to me has actually served to advance the gospel." (Philippians 1:12). Change becomes context, not obstacle. Believers are invited into this same flexibility. Faithful action continues even when original plans are no longer possible. God's will is not tied to a single method or outcome. It is expressed wherever believers remain obedient and trusting.

Letting go without losing hope

Disrupted plans often require letting go of deeply held hopes. The Bible acknowledges the grief this involves. Hope is not denied, but it is reshaped.

The psalmist prays, *"Whom have I in heaven but you? And earth has nothing I desire besides you."* (Psalm 73:25). This is not a rejection of earthly hopes, but a reordering of them. God remains the ultimate source of meaning and security.

Letting go does not mean resignation. It means trusting God to redefine the future. Believers can grieve what has been lost while remaining open to what God is doing next. Hope is not destroyed by change. It is refined.

A larger view of God's purposes

As believers step back from individual plans, the Bible invites them to view their lives within God's larger purposes. God is not merely guiding individual decisions. He is forming people, building His church, and advancing His kingdom.

Paul reminds believers, *"We are God's handiwork, created in Christ Jesus to do good works, which God prepared in advance for us to do."* (Ephesians 2:10).

These good works are not limited to specific plans. They unfold across changing seasons and circumstances.

This larger view prevents believers from tying their sense of purpose to a single path. God's will is broader than any one plan. It encompasses the whole of a believer's life in Christ.

Confidence in a faithful God

As this chapter concludes, the central reassurance becomes clear. Change does not signal that God has lost control or that His will has been missed. It often reveals the depth and resilience of His purposes.

Proverbs affirms this enduring confidence: *"Many are the plans in a person's heart, but it is the Lord's purpose that prevails."* (19:21).

God's purposes stand firm, even as human plans shift. This truth frees believers from fear when circumstances change. They can plan, act, adapt, and trust, knowing that God remains faithful.

His will is not fragile. It is active, purposeful, and secure.

When plans unravel, faith does not collapse. It deepens.

Believers learn to hold their lives with open hands, confident that the God who began His work in them continues to guide them faithfully through every change, shaping their lives according to His good and gracious will.

11. DISCERNING GOD'S WILL WITHOUT FEAR

By this stage of the journey, it should be clear that much of the anxiety surrounding God's will does not arise from the Bible itself, but from the way believers have been taught to approach it. Fear enters when God's will is treated as a fragile target to be hit, rather than a gracious reality to be lived within. The Bible consistently invites believers into a different posture, one marked by confidence, trust, and freedom.

I want to address that fear directly and explore how discernment is meant to function in the Christian life, not as a high-stakes guessing game, but as a settled, faithful practice grounded in God's character and promises.

Fear as the enemy of discernment

Fear is one of the greatest obstacles to healthy discernment. When believers are afraid of missing God's will, every decision becomes weighted with exaggerated consequence. Fear narrows vision, distorts priorities, and undermines trust.

The Bible repeatedly warns against allowing fear to govern the life of faith. Paul reminds Timothy in 2 Timothy 1:7, *"For the Spirit God gave us does not make us timid, but gives us power, love and self-discipline."* Fear-driven discernment is not the same as Spirit-driven discernment. The Spirit produces confidence rooted in God's faithfulness, not anxiety rooted in uncertainty.

Fear often masquerades as reverence. Believers may claim they are being cautious or spiritually sensitive, when in reality they are paralysed by the fear of making a wrong move. The Bible does not commend this posture. Again and again, God's people are called to courage, not because outcomes are guaranteed, but because God is trustworthy. *"Be strong and courageous... for the Lord your God will be with you wherever you go."* (Joshua 1:9).

When fear dominates discernment, believers focus more on avoiding error than on living faithfully. This shifts attention away from God's character and more toward self-protection. Discernment shaped by fear inevitably becomes distorted.

God's character as the foundation of discernment

Biblical discernment does not ever begin with decision-making techniques, but with confidence in who God is. The Bible consistently anchors faith in God's goodness, wisdom, and steadfast love. Without this foundation, discernment becomes fragile and unstable.

James speaks directly to this when he writes, *"If any of you lacks wisdom, you should ask God, who gives generously to all without finding fault."* (James 1:5). This promise dismantles fear. God is not reluctant, critical, or withholding. He delights to give wisdom. Discernment is not something believers must earn or unlock. It is a gift given by a generous God.

The psalms repeatedly return to this theme. *"The Lord is good to all; he has compassion on all he has made."* (Psalm 145:9). God's guidance flows from His goodness, not from a desire to test or trap His people. He does not hide His will to watch believers fail. He guides as a loving Father.

Jesus reinforces this confidence when He asks, *"Which of you, if your son asks for bread, will give him a stone?"* (Matthew 7:9). The implication is unmistakable. God does not mislead His children. He does not punish sincere faith with silence or confusion. Discernment rests securely on the goodness of God.

Freedom from the fear of missing God's will

One of the most persistent fears believers carry is the fear that God's will can be missed easily and irreversibly. The Bible offers no support for this idea. On the contrary, it repeatedly affirms God's ability to accomplish His purposes through imperfect people and imperfect choices.

Paul expresses this assurance with clarity: *"He who began a good work in you will carry it on to completion until the day of Christ Jesus."* (Philippians 1:6). God's work is not fragile. It is not dependent on flawless discernment. It is sustained by God's faithfulness over time. This truth frees believers from obsessive self-monitoring. They no longer need to scrutinise every decision as though everything hangs in the balance.

God's will is not a narrow path easily lost, but a secure purpose actively at work in their lives.

The Bible also reminds believers that God's will is ultimately concerned with transformation, not location or occupation. *"For those God foreknew he also predestined to be conformed to the image of his Son."* (Romans 8:29). This purpose cannot be derailed by ordinary decisions. It unfolds across the whole of life as believers walk with God.

Discernment as faithful living, not perfect knowing

When fear is removed, discernment begins to take its proper shape. It is no longer about achieving perfect certainty, but about living faithfully with the light we've already been given. The Bible consistently affirms this posture. *"Your word is a lamp for my feet, a light on my path."* (Psalm 119:105). A lamp illuminates the next step, not the entire journey.

God does not promise exhaustive knowledge of the future. He promises sufficient guidance for faithful obedience in the present. Discernment operates within that promise. Believers listen to the Bible, seek wisdom, pray honestly, and act responsibly. They trust God with what they cannot yet see.

This understanding dismantles the fear that has burdened so many believers. Discernment is not a spiritual minefield. It is a daily expression of trust. God's will is not something to fear or second-guess endlessly. It is the gracious context in which believers live, choose, and grow as they walk with a faithful and trustworthy God.

As fear loosens its grip, discernment becomes calmer, clearer, and more grounded. Believers begin to live not as anxious seekers of hidden answers, but as confident children trusting the God who leads them faithfully, step by step, within His good and perfect will.

As fear loosens its grip, discernment begins to function as the Bible intends. It becomes less reactive and more settled, less driven by urgency and more shaped by trust.

Discernment shaped by trust rather than anxiety

Anxiety will push believers to seek certainty before obedience. Trust allows them to act faithfully without needing everything resolved. The Bible commends the latter posture, as we see in Proverbs 3:5, *"Trust in the Lord with all your heart and lean not on your own understanding."* Trust will never mean we abandoning understanding, but it does mean will must refuse to make it the foundation of our confidence.

When anxiety dominates, discernment becomes fragile. Believers often second-guess themselves constantly, interpret normal uncertainty as spiritual failure, and struggle to move forward. The Bible offers a different rhythm. For example, *"You will keep in perfect peace those whose minds are steadfast, because they trust in you."* (Isaiah 26:3). Peace stabilises discernment by anchoring it in God's faithfulness.

This trust allows believers to hold decisions lightly. They plan, act, and adapt without panic. Discernment becomes a steady practice rather than an emergency response.

The role of wisdom in confident discernment

The Bible places wisdom at the heart of discernment. Wisdom does not eliminate uncertainty, but it enables believers to navigate it faithfully. *"The fear of the Lord is the beginning of wisdom."* (Proverbs 9:10). Reverence for God shapes judgement, priorities, and responses.

Paul prays that believers may grow in discernment through wisdom: *"That your love may abound more and more in knowledge and depth of insight."* (Philippians 1:9). Discernment grows as love, knowledge, and insight deepen together. It is relational and moral, not merely analytical.

Wisdom allows believers to evaluate decisions in light of the Bible, conscience, and impact on others. It asks whether choices are loving, faithful, and constructive. This kind of discernment does not require special revelation. It requires attentiveness to God's Word and openness to growth.

Learning to decide without absolute certainty

One of the hardest lessons for believers to embrace is that discernment does not guarantee certainty. The Bible never promises that faithful people will always feel sure. It calls them instead to always walk by faith. *"We live by faith, not by sight."* (2 Corinthians 5:7).

Biblical faith involves acting on sufficient light rather than trying to wait for clarity. The psalmist captures this posture: *"The Lord makes firm the steps of the one who delights in him."* (Psalm 37:23). Steps are taken one at a time. God directs movement, not speculation.

Learning to decide without absolute certainty is not recklessness. It is trust expressed through action. Believers move forward prayerfully, willing to learn, adjust, and grow. God's will is not thwarted by this process. It is worked out through it.

Discernment strengthened through experience

The Bible assumes that discernment deepens through lived experience. It is not static. It develops as believers engage life under God's Word. The writer to the Hebrews describes mature believers as those *"who by constant use have trained themselves to distinguish good from evil."* (Hebrews 5:14).

Experience will refine our discernment when it is reflected upon humbly. Success can teach gratitude, whereas difficulty teaches dependence. Both contribute to wisdom. God does not shield His people from learning through experience. He walks with them through it.

This perspective removes the fear of failure. Discernment is not proven by never needing correction. It is proven by remaining teachable. God's will is honoured as believers continue to listen, learn, and trust Him over time.

A steady confidence in God's leading

As discernment matures, confidence grows. This confidence is not self-assurance. It is assurance rooted in God's character. Believers trust that God is leading them faithfully, even when the path ahead is not fully visible.

The Psalmist expresses this confidence simply: *"The Lord will accomplish what concerns me."* (Psalm 138:8). God's purposes are not dependent on perfect discernment. They are carried forward by His steadfast love.

When discernment is freed from fear, it becomes a gift rather than a burden. Believers no longer approach decisions with dread, but with quiet confidence. They trust that as they live faithfully before God, His will is being worked out in their lives. In this way, discernment becomes not a source of anxiety, but a steady expression of faith. It reflects a deepening trust in the God who guides His people, not by fear or pressure, but by wisdom, love, and faithful presence.

As discernment becomes steadier and less fear-driven, it settles into a pattern that the Bible consistently commends: faithful living marked by trust, humility, and perseverance. I now want to draw those threads together, showing how discernment functions not as a momentary achievement, but as a lifelong posture before God.

Discernment sustained over time

The Bible evaluates discernment not by isolated decisions, but by the overall direction of someone's life. Faithfulness is measured in perseverance, not perfection. Paul reflects on his own life with this long view when he writes, *"I have fought the good fight, I have finished the race, I have kept the faith."* (2 Timothy 4:7). Discernment is proven across years of walking with God, not in the certainty of individual moments.

This perspective protects believers from unrealistic expectations. They are not called to get everything right immediately. They are called to remain faithful, responsive, and humble over time. God's will unfolds across seasons, through growth, correction, and grace.

Discernment matures as believers learn to recognise patterns in their lives. As wisdom deepens, decisions become less anxious and more instinctively aligned with God's character. This is not because believers become infallible, but because they become more deeply rooted in trust.

Living responsibly without fear of failure

Fear of failure often lurks beneath anxiety about God's will. Believers worry that a wrong decision will undo God's purposes or permanently sideline them. The Bible consistently dismantles this fear.

Peter's life offers a powerful example. His failures are public and painful, yet God restores him and entrusts him with great responsibility. God's purposes are never derailed by human weakness. They are often revealed through it, as Paul reminds us: *"My grace is sufficient for you, for my power is made perfect in weakness."* (2 Corinthians 12:9).

This truth allows believers to act responsibly without fear. They make decisions prayerfully, accept responsibility, and trust God with the outcome. When correction is needed, God provides it. Failure does not remove believers from God's will. It often deepens dependence on His grace.

Discernment anchored in God's faithfulness

At its core, discernment without fear rests on confidence in God's faithfulness. The Bible repeatedly affirms that God is committed to His people far more deeply than they are committed to making the right choices. Psalm 138:8 declares, *"The Lord will fulfil his purpose for me; your love, Lord, endures forever."* This assurance does not depend on clarity or control. It rests on God's steadfast love. God completes what He begins.

Paul echoes this conviction in Philippians 1:6, *"He who began a good work in you will carry it on to completion until the day of Christ Jesus."* Discernment operates within this security. Believers are not navigating life alone or at risk of falling outside God's care. They are held within His faithful purposes.

A life marked by trustful obedience

As fear recedes, discernment finds its proper expression in trustful obedience. Believers listen to the Bible, seek wisdom, pray honestly, and act faithfully. They do not wait for perfect certainty. They trust God as they walk.

The Bible captures this posture succinctly: *"Commit your way to the Lord; trust in him and he will do this."* (Psalm 37:5). Commitment and trust belong together. God's will is not something believers must uncover with precision. It is something they live within as they walk faithfully before Him.

When discernment is shaped this way, the Christian life becomes steadier and more confident. Decisions are made without panic. Adjustments are made without shame. Growth continues without fear. God's will is no longer a source of anxiety, but a context of grace.

In this light, discernment becomes what the Bible always intended it to be: a faithful, ongoing response to a trustworthy God. As believers live this way, they discover that God's will is not difficult to miss, nor dangerous to approach. It is the gracious and faithful purpose of a God who leads His people with patience, wisdom, and unfailing love.

12. GOD'S WILL AND THE SHAPE
OF A FAITHFUL LIFE

As we continue our study of God's will, the focus now shifts from individual moments of discernment to the overall shape of a faithful Christian life. Questions about God's will do not ultimately find their answer in isolated decisions, but in the direction, posture, and character of a life lived in Christ. The Bible consistently frames God's will in these broader terms.

This chapter explores how God's will is expressed not primarily through dramatic guidance or decisive moments, but through the steady formation of a life that reflects Christ. When this larger perspective is fully embraced, many of the anxieties surrounding God's will lose their grip.

God's will as a life direction, not a series of choices

One of the most important biblical shifts believers can make is moving from a decision-centred view of God's will to a direction-centred one. The Bible rarely treats God's will as a string of isolated instructions. Instead, it speaks of a path, a walk, or a way of life.

Paul urges believers, *"Live a life worthy of the calling you have received."* (Ephesians 4:1). This is not a command about a specific decision. It is a call to live in a manner shaped by the gospel. God's will is expressed through how believers live, not merely through what they decide.

The imagery of walking appears repeatedly in the Bible. *"Blessed are those whose ways are blameless, who walk according to the law of the Lord."* (Psalm 119:1).

A walk is continuous and it is relational. It assumes progress, growth, and occasional missteps, all within the context of an ongoing journey with God.

When God's will is understood in this way, it becomes less fragile. It is not lost with one wrong turn. It is lived out over time as believers continue walking faithfully with God.

Character formation at the heart of God's will

The Bible consistently places character at the centre of God's will. God is far more concerned with who believers are becoming than with the specific circumstances they occupy. This truth is explicit in the New Testament.

Paul states God's purpose plainly: *"For those God foreknew he also predestined to be conformed to the image of his Son."* (Romans 8:29). This is not a secondary aim. It is the overarching direction of God's will for every believer. Transformation into Christlikeness is not optional or incidental. It is central.

Peter echoes this emphasis when he writes, *"Just as he who called you is holy, so be holy in all you do."* (1 Peter 1:15). Holiness is not limited to moral behaviour. It encompasses attitudes, desires, and responses. God's will reaches into the deepest parts of a person's life.

When believers prioritise character formation, many decisions become much clearer. Choices are evaluated not merely by opportunity or preference, but by their capacity to foster faithfulness, humility, love, and obedience.

Faithfulness in ordinary life

Another consistent biblical theme is the value God places on ordinary faithfulness. The Bible does not suggest that God's will is reserved for extraordinary callings or dramatic acts of obedience. Much of God's will is worked out in the ordinary rhythms of daily life.

Paul encourages believers, *"Whatever you do, whether in word or deed, do it all in the name of the Lord Jesus."* (Colossians 3:17). God's will is not confined to major life decisions. It extends into work, relationships, service, and daily responsibilities.

Jesus reinforces this focus on ordinary faithfulness when He teaches that those who are faithful in small things can be trusted with greater things (Luke 16:10). God's will is often revealed not through spectacular guidance, but through consistent obedience in everyday contexts.

This perspective liberates believers from the pressure to identify a single defining moment that determines their faithfulness. God's will is then honoured in countless small acts of trust and obedience, repeated day after day.

Stability rooted in God's unchanging purpose

When God's will is framed as the shaping of a faithful life, it provides stability amid change. Circumstances may shift, roles may change, and plans may evolve, but God's purpose remains constant.

The writer of Hebrews reminds believers, *"Jesus Christ is the same yesterday and today and forever."* (Hebrews 13:8). Because God's character does not change, His purposes remain steady. Believers are not required to reinvent faithfulness with every new season of life.

This stability allows believers to face change without fear. They are free to adapt, grow, and respond to new circumstances, confident that God's will continues to shape them through it all. As believers anchor their understanding of God's will in the formation of a faithful life, they discover a deeper sense of peace. God's will is no longer something to locate anxiously, but something to live faithfully. It is expressed through a life shaped by Christ, sustained by grace, and marked by steady trust in the God who is always at work.

When God's will is understood as shaping the whole direction of a life, attention naturally turns to the practices and priorities that sustain that life over time. The Bible does not leave believers guessing here. It repeatedly identifies the habits, attitudes, and commitments through which God forms His people into the likeness of Christ.

The centrality of abiding in Christ

At the heart of a faithful life is an ongoing, living relationship with Christ. Jesus describes this relationship using the language of abiding: *"Remain in me, as I also remain in you."* (John 15:4). This command is not about achieving spiritual intensity, but about sustained connection. Fruitfulness flows from remaining, not from striving.

Jesus makes the relationship unmistakable: *"If you remain in me and I in you, you will bear much fruit; apart from me you can do nothing."* (John 15:5). God's will is not fulfilled through isolated acts of obedience detached from relationship. It is fulfilled through lives that remain rooted in Christ.

Abiding shapes discernment by anchoring it relationally. Decisions are never made in isolation, they are made within a living relationship that influences desires, values, and priorities. This relational focus protects believers from treating God's will as an abstract concept rather than a lived reality.

The Bible as the shape-setter of life

The Bible plays a decisive role in shaping a faithful life. The Bible is not merely a reference point for decision-making. It is the means by which God continually renews the mind and reshapes understanding.

Paul urges believers, *"Do not conform to the pattern of this world, but be transformed by the renewing of your mind."* (Romans 12:2). This transformation occurs as God's Word reshapes our thought patterns, our values, and our assumptions. This renewal enables discernment, allowing believers to *"test and approve what God's will is."* (Romans 12:2).

The Bible does not function as a rulebook for every situation. It forms character. As believers immerse themselves in God's Word, their instincts begin to align with God's will. Decisions increasingly flow from a renewed mind rather than from anxiety or pressure.

Prayer as ongoing dependence

Prayer sustains a faithful life by cultivating dependence on God. The Bible presents prayer not primarily as a tool for decision-making, but as a means of ongoing relationship and trust.

In 1 Thessalonians 5:17, we read where Paul exhorts all believers to *"pray continually."* This does not imply constant verbal prayer, but a posture of attentiveness and reliance. Prayer keeps believers oriented toward God as they move through daily life.

Through prayer, believers learn to entrust their concerns, desires, and uncertainties to God. *"Cast all your anxiety on him because he cares for you."* (1 Peter 5:7). Prayer shapes the heart, quiets fear and reinforces trust. It sustains faithfulness even when clarity is limited.

Community as God's context for formation

The Bible usually places spiritual growth within community. God's will is not worked out in isolation. Believers are formed together as they share life, truth, and accountability. The early church exemplifies this shared life: *"They devoted themselves to the apostles' teaching and to fellowship ..."* (Acts 2:42). Teaching and fellowship belong together. God uses relationships to shape our character, correct our blind spots, and encourage perseverance.

Community also provides a context for discernment. Wisdom is tested, refined, and strengthened through the counsel of others. *"Plans fail for lack of counsel, but with many advisers they succeed."* (Proverbs 20:18). God's will is very often clarified as believers listen to one another humbly.

Perseverance as the mark of a faithful life

A faithful life is marked not by intensity, but by perseverance. the Bible consistently honours endurance. God's will unfolds over time, often through steady faithfulness rather than dramatic moments.

In the book of Hebrews all believers are urged to *"run with perseverance the race marked out for us."* (Hebrews 12:1). The race is already marked. The task is to keep running. God's will is not discovered by constantly changing direction, but by staying the course in trust.

Perseverance guards against discouragement when growth feels slow or progress unclear. God is at work even when change is gradual. Faithfulness over time reveals the shape of God's will more clearly than isolated acts ever could. As these practices take root, believers begin to see how God's will is woven into the fabric of everyday life.

It is expressed through abiding in Christ, immersion in the Bible, ongoing prayer, shared community, and perseverance. Together, these shape a life that reflects God's purposes steadily and faithfully, even amid the ordinary and the unseen.

As the shape of a faithful life comes into view, the question of God's will is finally relocated to where the Bible consistently places it: not in anxious decision-making, but in a settled pattern of trustful obedience. God's will is not something believers step into occasionally. It is the environment in which they live as they walk with Him over time.

Faithfulness as the measure of a life

The Bible repeatedly measures faithfulness not by prominence, certainty, or success, but by perseverance in obedience. God's will is revealed most clearly not in moments of clarity, but in lives that remain steady through changing seasons.

Jesus' parable of the faithful servant highlights this perspective. The servant is commended not for brilliance or achievement, but for reliability: *"Well done, good and faithful servant! You have been faithful with a few things."* (Matthew 25:21). Faithfulness is measured over time, in ordinary responsibilities carried out with integrity.

This reframes how believers evaluate their lives. The question is not, "Have I discovered God's will?" but, "Am I living faithfully before God today?" the Bible consistently affirms that this kind of faithfulness honours God's will more deeply than anxious striving ever could.

God's will and the ordinary seasons of life

One of the quiet revelations of the Bible is how much of God's will is worked out in ordinary seasons. There are long stretches of biblical history where nothing dramatic appears to happen, yet God's purposes are steadily unfolding. Paul affirms this ordinary faithfulness when he writes, *"Make it your ambition to lead a quiet life."* (1 Thessalonians 4:11). God's will is not opposed to stability or routine. It is often expressed through consistency, responsibility, and quiet obedience.

This truth frees believers from the assumption that God's will must always feel significant or urgent. Much of a faithful life consists of showing up, loving well, working honestly, and trusting God in the small, unseen moments. These are not secondary to God's will. They are central to it.

Living with confidence in God's ongoing work

As believers embrace the shape of a faithful life, confidence grows. This confidence is not rooted in certainty about the future, but in assurance that God is actively at work in the present.

In Philippians 2:13, Paul expresses this assurance clearly: *"For it is God who works in you to will and to act according to his good purpose."* This confidence allows believers to live without fear of drifting outside God's purposes. God's will is not a narrow path easily lost. It is the steady work of a faithful God forming His people into the likeness of Christ across the whole of life.

A life resting in God's faithful care

When God's will is understood in this way, it becomes a source of peace rather than pressure. Believers no longer feel the need to constantly evaluate their position or question their standing. They rest in God's faithful care.

Jesus invites His followers into this rest when He says, *"Come to me, all you who are weary and burdened, and I will give you rest."* (Matthew 11:28). This rest is not passivity. It is confidence grounded in trust. God's will does not demand relentless effort. It invites faithful participation.

As believers live within this rest, obedience becomes more natural and less strained. Faithfulness flows from relationship rather than obligation. God's will is no longer something to chase or fear. It is the gracious context in which believers live, grow, and serve. In the end, the shape of a faithful life reveals the heart of God's will. It is a life rooted in Christ, formed by the Bible, sustained by prayer, strengthened in community, and marked by perseverance.

Such a life does not need constant reassurance because it rests confidently in the God who is faithful, purposeful, and present in every season.

13 FREEDOM, RESPONSIBILITY, AND LIVING WELL BEFORE GOD

Now it is time for one major tension to be addressed carefully and biblically: the relationship between Christian freedom and human responsibility. For many believers, freedom sounds dangerous and responsibility sounds burdensome. Yet the Bible holds these two together without embarrassment or apology. God's will is never honoured by fear-driven restraint, nor is it expressed through careless autonomy. It is lived out through responsible freedom before God.

Let us now explore how the Bible presents freedom not as a threat to faithfulness, but as the very context in which obedience, wisdom, and love flourish.

Freedom as a gift of grace

Christian freedom is not a concession or a risk God reluctantly allows. It is a gift secured by Christ and central to the gospel itself. Paul states this without qualification: *"It is for freedom that Christ has set us free."* (Galatians 5:1). Freedom is not peripheral to salvation. It is one of its defining outcomes.

This freedom is first and foremost the complete freedom from condemnation. *"Therefore, there is now no condemnation for those who are in Christ Jesus."* (Romans 8:1). Believers are no longer living under the threat of rejection or divine displeasure. God's acceptance is settled in Christ. This truth radically reshapes how decisions are should be approached. Fear loses its power when condemnation is removed.

Freedom is also the freedom from the tyranny of rule-based righteousness. Paul warns against returning to a mindset that measures faithfulness by external compliance rather than inward transformation. *"If you are led by the Spirit, you are not under the law."* (Galatians 5:18). This does not abolish moral boundaries. It relocates obedience from compulsion to relationship. When freedom is understood as grace, it ceases to be threatening. It becomes the space in which believers live securely before God, free to grow, learn, and respond without fear.

Responsibility as the shape of mature freedom

The Bible never presents freedom as irresponsibility. On the contrary, freedom is the condition in which responsibility becomes meaningful. Paul holds these together clearly: *"You were called to be free. But do not use your freedom to indulge the flesh; rather, serve one another humbly in love."* (Galatians 5:13).

Freedom does not remove responsibility. It intensifies it. Believers are now responsible not out of fear of punishment, but out of love for God and others. This shift marks spiritual maturity. Immature faith seeks rules to avoid error. Mature faith embraces responsibility as an expression of trust.

Responsibility means recognising that choices matter. The Bible affirms this repeatedly. *"Each of you should test your own actions."* (Galatians 6:4). Believers are called to thoughtful self-examination, not anxious self-surveillance. Responsibility will involve reflection, honesty, and the willingness to learn.

This understanding guards against two extremes. It prevents freedom from becoming self-indulgence, and it also prevents responsibility from becoming legalism. Both distort God's will. The Bible holds them together as complementary realities.

God's will and the call to wise living

One of the ways the Bible connects freedom and responsibility is through its emphasis on wisdom. God does not replace wisdom with commands for every situation. He calls His people to live wisely within the freedom He provides.

Paul urges believers in Ephesians 5:15–16, to *"be very careful, then, how you live – not as unwise but as wise, making the most of every opportunity."*

Wisdom is attentive, responsive, and grounded in God's truth. It does not require certainty about outcomes. It requires faithfulness in action. Wisdom recognises context, consequence, and impact. It asks not only what is permitted, but what is beneficial. *"'I have the right to do anything,' you say – but not everything is beneficial."* (1 Corinthians 6:12). Freedom creates choice. Wisdom evaluates it.

Living wisely honours God's will precisely because it takes responsibility seriously. Believers are not passive recipients of direction. They are active participants in a life shaped by God's truth and grace.

Freedom that serves love

The Bible ultimately frames freedom around love. Love is the goal, the measure, and the boundary of Christian freedom. Paul makes this unmistakably clear in Galatians 5:14. He writes, *"The entire law is fulfilled in keeping this one command: 'Love your neighbour as yourself.'"*

Freedom finds its fullest expression not in self-expression, but in self-giving. Responsible freedom seeks the good of others, reflects Christ's humility, and builds up rather than tears down. This orientation reshapes how decisions are made. Choices are evaluated not merely by personal preference, but by their capacity to express love.

Jesus embodies this freedom perfectly. His life is marked by complete freedom and complete obedience. *"The Son of Man did not come to be served, but to serve"* (Mark 10:45). In Christ, freedom and responsibility are not in tension. They are united.

As believers learn to live within this union, God's will becomes clearer and more liveable. Freedom no longer feels dangerous. Responsibility no longer feels oppressive. Together, they form the framework of a faithful life lived confidently before God, shaped by grace, wisdom, and love. So when freedom and responsibility are held together biblically, the Christian life begins to take on a healthier tone. Believers are neither burdened by constant self-doubt nor tempted to adopt a very careless independence. Instead, the Bible calls them to live attentively, wisely, and lovingly within the freedom God has given.

Living responsibly without returning to legalism

One of the persistent dangers in emphasising responsibility is the subtle return of legalism. Believers may begin to measure faithfulness by performance, outcomes, or rigid self-imposed standards. The Bible consistently warns against this drift.

Paul confronts this tendency directly when he asks, *"After beginning by means of the Spirit, are you now trying to finish by means of the flesh?"* (Galatians 3:3). Responsibility that disconnects from grace becomes exhausting and ultimately destructive. God's will is not fulfilled through self-reliance masquerading as obedience.

Responsible living flows from identity, not anxiety. Believers obey because they belong to God, not so they can secure His approval. *"You are not your own; you were bought at a price."* (1 Corinthians 6:19–20). Responsibility arises from gratitude and love, not fear of failure. This protects believers from turning discernment into self-surveillance. They are called to live thoughtfully, not to constantly monitor themselves for spiritual error. God's will is honoured when responsibility remains rooted in grace.

Freedom guided by love and conscience

The Bible repeatedly teaches that freedom must be guided by love and informed by conscience. Paul addresses this clearly when discussing disputable matters within the church. *"You, then, why do you judge your brother or sister? ... Each of us will give an account of ourselves to God."* (Romans 14:10–12).

Freedom does not eliminate accountability. Believers remain responsible for how their choices affect others. Paul urges sensitivity: *"Make up your mind not to put any stumbling block or obstacle in the way of a brother or sister."* (Romans 14:13). Love restrains freedom without negating it.

Conscience also plays a vital role here. The Bible affirms the importance of acting with integrity before God. *"Blessed is the one who does not condemn himself by what he approves."* (Romans 14:22). Decisions should be made honestly, without inner compromise or pressure to conform. Living well before God involves listening to conscience shaped by the Bible, guided by love, and exercised in freedom.

Wisdom in the use of freedom

Freedom always presents options. Wisdom evaluates them. the Bible repeatedly affirms that not every permissible choice is wise or constructive.

Paul's words are stark in 1 Corinthians 6:12, *"'I have the right to do anything,' you say – but not everything is beneficial."* Wisdom asks how choices shape character, relationships, and witness. It looks beyond immediate gratification to long-term fruit.

You will notice the book of Proverbs consistently links wisdom with foresight. *"The wise see danger and take refuge, but the simple keep going and pay the penalty."* (Proverbs 27:12). This is not fear-based restraint, but thoughtful responsibility. Wisdom honours God by recognising that freedom carries weight.

Believers are encouraged to grow in this kind of wisdom over time. *"Let the wise listen and add to their learning."* (Proverbs 1:5). God's will is lived out as believers become increasingly skilled at using freedom well.

Accountability without control

The Bible values accountability, but it never confuses it with control. God's will is never advanced through domination or coercion, but through mutual encouragement and shared responsibility.

Paul urges believers to *"carry each other's burdens"* (Galatians 6:2), while also affirming that *"each one should carry their own load."* (Galatians 6:5). These statements are not contradictory. They describe a balanced community where support and responsibility coexist.

Healthy accountability always encourages growth without undermining freedom. It creates space for honest conversation, correction, and encouragement. It does not replace personal responsibility, nor does it demand uniformity of decision-making.

God's will is honoured as our faith is expressed through love, humility, and mutual care. As freedom and responsibility continue to shape daily life, believers discover that God's will is neither oppressive nor permissive. It is purposeful. It invites them to live thoughtfully and generously before God, trusting that the freedom He gives is sufficient and the responsibility He calls for is both meaningful and life-giving.

As freedom and responsibility share a proper relationship, the Christian life takes on a distinctive quality. It becomes neither anxious nor careless, neither rigid nor vague. The Bible presents this way of living as mature, grounded, and deeply honouring to God. The focus now turns to how freedom and responsibility are sustained together over the long course of life.

Living before God rather than before fear

One of the clearest signs that freedom and responsibility are rightly held together is the absence of fear. When believers live under fear, responsibility becomes oppressive and freedom feels dangerous. The Bible calls believers to live before God instead.

Paul captures this orientation when he writes, *"We make it our goal to please him."* (2 Corinthians 5:9). Living to please God is not driven by anxiety about consequences. It is motivated by relationship. Believers act responsibly because they care about honouring the One who loves them.

The Bible repeatedly contrasts fear-based living with trust-based obedience. *"There is no fear in love. But perfect love drives out fear."* (1 John 4:18). Fear distorts discernment and burdens responsibility. Love steadies both. When believers live before God rather than before fear, their decisions become freer and more faithful.

Responsibility as participation in God's work

The Bible presents responsibility not as a burden imposed by God, but as participation in what He is already doing. Believers are invited to share in God's purposes through faithful action.

Paul expresses this partnership clearly: *"We are co-workers in God's service."* (1 Corinthians 3:9). Responsibility flows from dignity. God entrusts His people with real choices because He values them and involves them in His work.

Responsibility is not a sign of distance from God, but of a genuine relationship with Him. This understanding completely transforms how responsibility is experienced.

Decisions are no longer heavy because everything depends on getting them right. They are meaningful because they are taken up into God's larger purposes. God remains sovereign, yet believers are genuinely involved.

Freedom that endures through change

True Christian freedom is not fragile. It does not disappear when circumstances shift or when life becomes complex. The Bible consistently presents freedom as something that endures because it is grounded in Christ, not in conditions.

Paul affirms this enduring freedom when he writes, *"Where the Spirit of the Lord is, there is freedom."* (2 Corinthians 3:17). This freedom is not tied to outcomes or stability. It remains present in change, uncertainty, and also in difficulty. Because this freedom endures, believers then are able to remain responsible without becoming rigid. They can adapt, learn, and adjust without fear of falling outside God's will. Freedom gives them room to grow. Responsibility gives them direction.

A life that reflects God's wisdom and grace

When freedom and responsibility are lived together over time, the result is a life that reflects both God's wisdom and His grace. The Bible consistently portrays this as the mark of maturity.

Paul urges believers, *"Let your conversation be always full of grace, seasoned with salt."* (Colossians 4:6). Grace and wisdom are not opposed. A life shaped by both does not need constant rules or constant reassurance. It is guided by love, truth, and trust in God. Such a life honours God's will quietly but profoundly. It does not seek attention. It does not strive for certainty. It walks faithfully, making real choices with humility and confidence.

In the end, freedom and responsibility are not competing forces in the Christian life. They are God's gifts, given together. Freedom secures believers in God's grace. Responsibility invites them to live meaningfully within it. When held together, they form the framework of a life lived well before God, shaped by trust, guided by wisdom, and sustained by the faithful love of the One who calls His people to walk with Him.

14. GOD'S WILL, SUFFERING, AND THE QUESTIONS THAT REMAIN

No discussion of God's will would be complete unless we can address suffering. For many believers, questions about God's will do not arise in moments of choice, but in moments of pain. It is often suffering, loss, illness, disappointment, or unanswered prayer that drives people back to this question with renewed urgency: *If God has a will, how does this fit?* The Bible does not avoid this question, nor does it offer simplistic answers. Instead, it provides a framework that allows believers to hold faith, pain, and trust together without denial or despair.

Suffering is not outside God's will, yet not easily explained

One of the most difficult tensions the Bible asks believers to hold is this: suffering is neither outside God's sovereignty nor easily explained by it. The Bible consistently affirms that God reigns, even in a broken world, while also refusing to attribute suffering to simple moral or spiritual formulas.

Job's story is foundational here. Job suffers profoundly, yet the Bible explicitly rejects the idea that his suffering is the result of personal sin or poor discernment.

God Himself declares, *"There is no one on earth like him; he is blameless and upright."* (Job 1:8). Job's suffering is real, severe, and unexplained. The Bible does not rush to justify it.

This alone dismantles a common assumption: that if we are suffering, we must have missed God's will. The Bible does not support that conclusion. Faithful people suffer. Obedient people suffer. Godly people suffer. Suffering is not proof of spiritual failure, nor is it evidence that God's will has been abandoned.

At the same time, the Bible does not portray suffering as meaningless chaos. God remains sovereign, even when His purposes are hidden. *"The Lord gave and the Lord has taken away; may the name of the Lord be praised."* (Job 1:21). This statement does not explain suffering. It affirms trust in the midst of it.

Jesus and the will of God in the midst of suffering

The clearest revelation of God's will in relation to suffering is found in Jesus Christ. If suffering were evidence of being outside God's will, the life of Jesus would make no sense. His obedience leads directly to suffering, rejection, and death.

Jesus is explicit about this. *"The Son of Man must suffer many things and be rejected."* (Luke 9:22). The word *must* is crucial. Suffering is not an accident in Jesus' life. It is woven into God's redemptive purpose. Yet the Bible never suggests that God delights in suffering for its own sake.

In Gethsemane, Jesus prays with honesty and anguish: *"My Father, if it is possible, may this cup be taken from me. Yet not as I will, but as you will."* (Matthew 26:39). This amazing prayer shows us something essential. Submitting to God's will does not require emotional detachment or stoic acceptance. Jesus grieves, pleads, and suffers, while still entrusting Himself to the Father.

This moment reframes how believers understand God's will in suffering. God's will does not eliminate pain. It sustains faith within it. Obedience does not shield believers from sorrow. It anchors them in trust when sorrow comes.

Suffering and the myth of a pain-free path

Much confusion about God's will arises from an unbiblical expectation that obedience leads to ease. The Bible consistently dismantles this myth. Jesus Himself warns His followers, *"In this world you will have trouble."* (John 16:33). This is not a failure of God's will. It is part of life in a fallen world.

Paul echoes this realism when he writes, *"We must go through many hardships to enter the kingdom of God."* (Acts 14:22). Hardship is not a detour from God's purposes. It is often the terrain through which those purposes unfold.

This does not mean believers should seek suffering or minimise it. The Bible never glorifies pain. It acknowledges it honestly. The psalms give voice to anguish, confusion, and protest. *"How long, Lord? Will you forget me forever?"* (Psalm 13:1).

Such prayers are not faithless. They are faithful responses to real suffering. Recognising that suffering can exist within God's will frees believers from crushing self-blame. When hardship comes, the question is not, *Where did I go wrong?* but, *How do I trust God here?*

God's will as faithfulness, not explanation

Perhaps the hardest lesson the Bible teaches about suffering is that God does not always explain Himself. He does not provide neat answers that resolve pain. Instead, He offers His presence.

At the end of Job's story, God does not explain Job's suffering. He reveals Himself. *"Where were you when I laid the earth's foundation?"* (Job 38:4). This is not a rebuke. It is a reorientation. Job is invited to trust God's wisdom rather than demand understanding.

This pattern appears again and again in the Bible. God's will is not primarily about explanation, but about faithfulness. *"Even though I walk through the darkest valley, I will fear no evil, for you are with me."* (Psalm 23:4). The promise is not clarity. It is presence.

For believers, this is both sobering and comforting. God's will does not guarantee that suffering will make sense. It guarantees that God will be present, faithful, and trustworthy within it.

As this chapter unfolds, it will become clear that suffering does not contradict God's will, nor does it define it fully. Instead, suffering becomes one of the places where trust is refined, faith is deepened, and God's faithfulness is known not through answers, but through His sustaining grace.

If suffering is not evidence that God's will has been missed, the next question believers naturally ask is this: *What is God doing through it?*

The Bible approaches this question with great care. It does not offer a single explanation for suffering, nor does it reduce pain to a lesson or a test. Instead, it reveals several ways God works faithfully within suffering, without diminishing its reality.

God's will at work without minimising pain

One of the most damaging responses to suffering is spiritual minimisation. Well-meaning believers may rush to explain pain as "for the best" or "part of God's plan" without acknowledging the depth of loss or grief. The Bible never does this. It allows suffering to be named, lamented, and felt. The psalms are especially instructive here. They refuse to rush past pain. "My tears have been my food day and night." (Psalm 42:3). This is not a theological statement. It is an honest expression of anguish. The Bible includes it without correction or qualification.

At the same time, the Bible affirms that God is at work even when pain is unresolved. Paul writes, "Therefore we do not lose heart. Though outwardly we are wasting away, yet inwardly we are being renewed day by day." (2 Corinthians 4:16). Notice the tension. Renewal does not cancel deterioration. God's work does not erase suffering. It coexists with it. This balance matters deeply. God's will does not require believers to pretend that suffering is manageable or meaningful in the moment. It invites them to trust that God is faithful even when suffering feels overwhelming and unanswered.

The shaping work of God through suffering

The Bible does speak about the shaping work God does through suffering, but it does so carefully. Suffering is never described as good in itself. It is described as something God uses without wasting. In Romans 5:3-4, Paul articulates this with both honesty and hope: "We also glory in our sufferings, because we know that suffering produces perseverance; perseverance, character; and character, hope." This is not triumphalism. It is realism rooted in faith. The chain Paul describes unfolds over time, not instantly. Suffering does not immediately produce hope. It produces endurance, which God then uses to shape character.

Peter echoes this perspective when he writes, "Though now for a little while you may have had to suffer grief in all kinds of trials." (1 Peter 1:6). The phrase had to does not imply that God delights in suffering, but that suffering exists within a larger redemptive context God is faithfully overseeing.

This shaping work does not mean every painful experience leads to visible growth. The Bible never promises that. It promises instead that God is able to work faithfully within suffering to deepen trust, refine faith, and draw believers closer to Himself.

When God's will feels hidden in suffering

One of the most honest admissions the Bible makes is that God's will often feels hidden in seasons of suffering. Believers may search for meaning and find none. The Bible validates this experience rather than correcting it. The lament psalms repeatedly voice this hiddenness. *"Why, Lord, do you stand far off? Why do you hide yourself in times of trouble?"* (Psalm 10:1). This question is not answered with explanation. It is answered with continued relationship. The psalmist keeps praying.

In Matthew 27:46, we see that even Jesus experiences this sense of abandonment on the cross. *"My God, my God, why have you forsaken me?"* This cry does not negate God's will. It reveals the depth of Christ's identification with human suffering. God's redemptive work is unfolding precisely where God feels most absent.

For believers, this means that feeling distant from God in suffering does not mean God is distant. It means suffering distorts perception. Faith in these moments is not clarity, but clinging.

Trusting God when answers do not come

Perhaps the hardest dimension of suffering is learning to trust God without answers. The Bible does not promise that suffering will be explained in this life. It promises instead that God is trustworthy.

In 2 Thessalonians 3:3, the Apostle Paul captures this trust with simple confidence: *"The Lord is faithful, and he will strengthen you and protect you."* Faith in suffering rests not on understanding God's purposes, but on trusting His character. This trust is not passive. It is active perseverance. Believers continue to pray, obey, love, and hope, even when clarity remains absent. *"Let us not become weary in doing good, for at the proper time we will reap a harvest if we do not give up"* (Galatians 6:9).

God's will in suffering is not that believers explain their pain, but that they are sustained within it. He remains present, faithful, and at work in ways that often cannot be seen or measured. Suffering does not sit outside God's will, nor does it fully reveal it. Instead, suffering becomes one of the places where faith is stripped of illusion, trust is deepened, and God's presence is known not through answers, but through endurance, grace, and hope that holds fast even when the questions remain.

As believers live through suffering, the most enduring questions often remain unanswered. The Bible does not resolve this tension by offering explanations, but by reframing hope. God's will in suffering is not ultimately revealed through understanding, but through redemption, presence, and the promise of restoration.

God's will and the hope beyond suffering

The Bible consistently anchors hope beyond the present experience of pain. It does not deny suffering, but it refuses to allow suffering to have the final word. Paul writes with quiet confidence, *"For our light and momentary troubles are achieving for us an eternal glory that far outweighs them all."* (2 Corinthians 4:17). This is not a denial of pain. It is a declaration of perspective shaped by eternity.

Christian hope does not claim that suffering will always be resolved in this life. It rests in the promise that suffering will not define the final outcome. God's will includes restoration, renewal, and resurrection. *"He will wipe every tear from their eyes. There will be no more death or mourning or crying or pain."* (Revelation 21:4). This promise does not explain present suffering, but it assures believers that it is not permanent.

Hope reorients faith away from immediate answers and toward ultimate trust. God's will is larger than any single season of pain. It encompasses a future in which suffering is finally undone.

God's presence as the heart of His will

If suffering strips away easy answers, it also clarifies what matters most. Again and again, the Bible returns to this truth: God's presence is the heart of His will for His people.

Isaiah speaks God's promise into fear and suffering: *"When you pass through the waters, I will be with you… When you walk through the fire, you will not be burned."* (Isaiah 43:2). The promise is not escape, but accompaniment. God does not guarantee a pain-free path. He guarantees His presence within it. This theme runs throughout the New Testament as well. Paul assures believers in 2 Timothy 4:17, *"The Lord stood by me and gave me strength."* God's will is not fulfilled by removing every hardship, but by sustaining His people through them.

For believers, this reshapes how suffering is interpreted. God's will is not measured by comfort or ease. It is measured by faithfulness and presence. Even in silence, even in pain, God remains near.

Suffering and the formation of Christlike hope

The Bible also reveals that suffering has a formative role in shaping Christlike hope. This does not make suffering desirable, but it makes it meaningful within God's redemptive purposes.

Paul writes, *"We know that the whole creation has been groaning as in the pains of childbirth."* (Romans 8:22). Groaning is not meaningless noise. It is the sound of longing for redemption. Believers share in this groaning as they wait for what God has promised. This hope is deeply Christ-centred. Jesus' suffering does not end in the cross. It leads to resurrection. *"Christ suffered once for sins… to bring you to God."* (1 Peter 3:18). The pattern of suffering followed by glory is not only Christ's story. It shapes the believer's hope as well.

Suffering, then, becomes one of the places where hope is refined. It teaches believers to long not merely for relief, but for restoration. God's will is not simply to help His people cope with suffering, but to lead them toward a future where suffering no longer exists.

Trusting God when the questions remain

Even as hope grows, questions often remain. The Bible does not demand that believers resolve every tension. It invites them instead to trust God with what they cannot yet understand.

Proverbs offers this quiet counsel: *"Trust in the Lord with all your heart and lean not on your own understanding."* (Proverbs 3:5). Trust does not require explanation. It requires confidence in God's character. This trust is not naïve. It is grounded in God's faithfulness revealed throughout the Bible and supremely in Christ.

Job's story ends not with answers, but with worship. *"My ears had heard of you but now my eyes have seen you."* (Job 42:5). Encounter replaces explanation. Presence replaces certainty. This is not a lesser resolution. It is a deeper one.

God's will as faithful love in a broken world

At this point in our study, one truth stands firm. God's will does not promise a life without suffering. It promises a God who is faithful within it. God's will is not fragile or thwarted by pain. It is expressed through love that endures, hope that sustains, and grace that redeems.

Paul captures this assurance with confidence: *"Nothing... will be able to separate us from the love of God that is in Christ Jesus our Lord."* (Romans 8:39). Suffering cannot sever that love. Silence cannot diminish it. Questions cannot undo it.

For believers, this becomes the deepest comfort. God's will is not a puzzle to solve in suffering. It is a relationship to trust. Even when answers remain elusive, God remains faithful.

In this light, suffering does not sit outside God's will, nor does it define it. It becomes one of the places where God's faithful love is most deeply known, not through explanation, but through presence, endurance, and the hope that one day all suffering will give way to redemption.

15. GOD'S WILL, SUCCESS, FAILURE, AND FAITHFULNESS

Few things shape a believer's understanding of God's will more powerfully than experiences of success and failure. When life appears to go well, it is tempting to assume that God's will is being fulfilled. When things fall apart, many conclude that something must have gone wrong. The Bible challenges both assumptions when it refuses to measure God's will by visible outcomes and instead calls believers to evaluate their lives through the lens of faithfulness.

This chapter explores how the Bible reframes success and failure, not as indicators of divine approval or disapproval, but as contexts in which God's will is lived out faithfully over time.

The Bible's surprising view of success

The Bible often defines success in ways that run counter to human instinct. Cultural measures of success tend to focus on achievement, recognition, growth, or influence. The Bible consistently shifts attention elsewhere.

Jesus makes this unmistakably clear in Mark 8:36 when He says, *"What good is it for someone to gain the whole world, yet forfeit their soul?"* Success that ignores faithfulness is hollow. God's will is not fulfilled by accumulation, prominence, or even visible effectiveness. It is fulfilled by obedience rooted in trust.

The Old Testament provides many examples of this inverted logic. The prophets of old are frequently rejected, ignored, or persecuted, yet the Bible affirms their faithfulness. Jeremiah's ministry produces little visible fruit by human standards, yet he is described as obedient to God's calling. Success, in God's economy, is not measured by response, but by faithfulness to the task given.

Jesus' own ministry reinforces this truth. He attracts crowds, but He also watches many turn away. He is misunderstood, opposed, and ultimately crucified.

Yet the Bible presents His life as the perfect fulfilment of God's will. *"I have brought you glory on earth by finishing the work you gave me to do."* (John 17:4). Faithfulness, not outcome, defines success.

Failure reconsidered in the light of God's will

Just as the Bible reshapes success, it radically reframes failure. Many believers interpret failure as evidence that they have stepped outside God's will. The Bible does not support this conclusion. Peter's denial of Jesus is a striking example. By any human measure, it is a profound failure. Yet Jesus does not discard Peter or redefine God's purposes because of it. Instead, He restores Peter and entrusts him with responsibility. *"Feed my sheep."* (John 21:17). Failure does not nullify calling. It often becomes the place where humility and dependence are formed.

The Bible consistently shows that God works through flawed people and imperfect choices. Abraham falters in faith. Moses strikes the rock in frustration. David commits grievous sin. None of these failures are celebrated, but neither do they derail God's redemptive purposes. God's will is not undone by human weakness.

This truth frees believers from interpreting every setback as spiritual catastrophe. Failure may require repentance, learning, or correction, but it does not automatically indicate that God's will has been abandoned. Often, God is at work in failure, refining character and deepening trust.

Faithfulness as the true measure

If success and failure are unreliable indicators, what does the Bible offer instead? Again and again, it points to faithfulness. Faithfulness is the steady commitment to trust and obey God regardless of outcomes. Paul articulates this clearly when he writes, *"Now it is required that those who have been given a trust must prove faithful"* (1 Corinthians 4:2).

Faithfulness is measured by response, not result. Believers are accountable for obedience, not for controlling outcomes. This understanding removes a very heavy burden. Believers are not responsible for guaranteeing success.

They are responsible for remaining faithful. God remains sovereign over what their faithfulness produces. Faithfulness also allows believers to live honestly with both success and failure. Success becomes a reason for gratitude, not pride. Failure becomes a place for humility, not despair. In both, God's will continues to be lived out.

When success becomes a spiritual test

The Bible also warns that success itself can become a spiritual test. Prosperity and influence often tempt believers to trust outcomes rather than God.

Moses warns Israel of this danger in Deuteronomy 8:12, *"When you eat and are satisfied... be careful that you do not forget the Lord."* Success can dull dependence. It can create the illusion that faithfulness is measured by visible blessing.

Paul echoes this warning when he writes, *"I know what it is to be in need, and I know what it is to have plenty."* (Philippians 4:12). Both abundance and lack require trust. God's will is not easier to live out in success than in failure. Both expose the heart.

Understanding this protects believers from equating success with God's approval. God's will is not validated by applause or growth. It is validated by trustful obedience.

A steadier way forward

As this chapter begins to unfold, a clearer picture emerges. God's will is not a scoreboard. It is a relationship. Success and failure are real experiences, but they are not ultimate measures of faithfulness.

The Bible invites believers to live with a steadier confidence. They are free to pursue excellence without idolising success. They are free to acknowledge failure without despair. In both, God remains faithful, present, and at work. Faithfulness becomes the guiding principle. Believers live responsibly, trust God with outcomes, and rest in the assurance that God's will is being fulfilled not through flawless performance, but through lives that remain anchored in trust, humility, and obedience before Him.

If faithfulness rather than outcome is the biblical measure, then success and failure must be re-examined not only individually, but in how they shape the long course of a believer's life. The Bible consistently warns that both can become distortions if they are allowed to define identity, worth, or confidence before God.

When success distorts discernment

One of the subtle dangers of success is that it can begin to function as confirmation. Believers may assume that because something is working, growing, or being affirmed, it must automatically reflect God's will. The Bible urges far greater caution.

Jesus warns against this kind of false confidence when He says, *"Many will say to me on that day, 'Lord, Lord, did we not prophesy in your name…?' Then I will tell them plainly, 'I never knew you.'"* (Matthew 7:22–23). The issue here is not activity or effectiveness, but relationship. Success can mask spiritual drift if it replaces dependence on God.

Paul expresses similar caution regarding ministry itself. *"So then, no more boasting about human leaders!"* (1 Corinthians 3:21). Growth and effectiveness are real, but they do not belong to those who experience them. *"So neither the one who plants nor the one who waters is anything, but only God, who makes things grow"* (1 Corinthians 3:7).

Success, then, must be held humbly. It is received with gratitude, not assumed as proof of superior discernment or divine favour. God's will is not confirmed by momentum alone.

When failure becomes a false verdict

Failure carries its own distortions. Where success tempts believers toward pride, failure tempts them toward condemnation. Many believers interpret failure as God's verdict on their worth, calling, or usefulness. The Bible consistently rejects this interpretation. Paul confronts this mindset very firmly: *"Who are you to judge someone else's servant? To their own master, servants stand or fall."* (Romans 14:4). God alone evaluates faithfulness. Failure in a task does not equal failure as a servant.

The Bible also reminds believers that God often works most deeply in seasons that feel unproductive or unsuccessful. Elijah's despair follows one of his greatest victories, yet in 1 Kings 19, God meets him not with rebuke, but with rest and gentle reassurance. Failure and exhaustion do not disqualify believers from God's care. Understanding this prevents failure from becoming a final judgment. It becomes a moment within a longer story of grace, learning, and continued faithfulness.

God's will and the long view of a life

The Bible consistently evaluates faithfulness across the whole of life rather than in isolated seasons. God's will is not revealed in a single success or failure, but in the overall direction of a person's walk with Him.

Paul reflects this perspective when he writes, *"I do not consider myself yet to have taken hold of it. But one thing I do... I press on toward the goal."* (Philippians 3:13–14). Even near the end of his ministry, Paul does not rest on past success or dwell on past failure. He remains oriented toward faithfulness.

This long view guards believers against drawing premature conclusions about God's will. Seasons change. Roles change. Capacity changes. God's purposes continue unfolding through all of it. Faithfulness is measured not by consistency of outcome, but by persistence of trust.

Faithfulness when results are mixed

Most believers live in the tension of mixed results. Some efforts bear fruit. Others do not. The Bible prepares believers for this reality without discouragement.

Jesus' parable of the sower makes this explicit. The same seed produces different results depending on conditions beyond the sower's control (Matthew 13:3–9). The sower's task is not to guarantee harvest, but to sow faithfully. Outcomes belong to God. This perspective frees believers from the burden of needing to make everything work. They act responsibly, invest faithfully, and entrust results to God. Success does not inflate their sense of calling. Failure does not negate it.

Paul summarises this posture simply: *"Therefore, my dear brothers and sisters, stand firm. Let nothing move you. Always give yourselves fully to the work of the Lord."* (1 Corinthians 15:58). Faithfulness remains the constant, regardless of visible return.

Confidence rooted beyond achievement

As believers grow in this understanding, confidence shifts away from achievement and toward God's faithfulness. Their sense of worth becomes anchored not in what they accomplish, but in who they are in Christ.

The Bible affirms this identity very clearly: *"You are God's workmanship, created in Christ Jesus."* (Ephesians 2:10). Believers are valued not because of what they produce, but because of who they belong to. Good works follow identity; they do not create it.

This reorientation stabilises the Christian life. Success becomes a gift to steward. Failure becomes a place to learn. Neither becomes the final word. God's will is lived out steadily as believers remain faithful, trusting that God is at work across the whole span of their lives, shaping them not through outcomes alone, but through enduring relationship, grace, and purpose.

As success and failure are held within a biblical framework, a deeper and more liberating truth emerges. God's will is not primarily revealed in what believers achieve or avoid, but in who they become as they walk faithfully with Him. The Bible consistently points beyond outcomes to endurance, trust, and hope that rests securely in God's character.

Faithfulness that outlasts seasons

The Bible teaches that faithfulness is proven over time, not in isolated moments. Seasons of success and failure come and go, but God's will is worked out through perseverance that remains anchored in trust.

The writer to the Hebrews urges believers, *"You need to persevere so that when you have done the will of God, you will receive what he has promised"* (Hebrews 10:36). Perseverance assumes difficulty. It assumes moments when obedience does not appear to pay off.

God's will is not fulfilled by short bursts of faith, but by steady endurance. Paul's life reflects this long obedience. Near the end of his ministry, he does not catalogue achievements or measure influence. In 2 Timothy 4:7, he simply affirms, *"I have kept the faith."* Faithfulness remains the defining marker, not success as the world defines it. This long view frees believers from the pressure to evaluate God's will too quickly. Faithfulness unfolds over years, often in ways that only become clear in hindsight.

Learning contentment in all outcomes

The Bible also presents contentment as a vital expression of faithfulness. Contentment does not mean indifference or lack of desire. It means trusting God regardless of circumstances.

Paul speaks quite candidly about this learned posture: *"I have learned to be content whatever the circumstances."* (Philippians 4:11). Contentment is not instinctive. It is learned through experience with both abundance and need. God's will is not measured by which of these a believer is experiencing, but by whether trust is sustained within them.

Contentment guards believers against interpreting success as entitlement or failure as punishment. It anchors joy in God rather than in outcomes. This allows believers to live faithfully without being controlled by circumstance.

God's will as participation, not performance

One of the most freeing insights the Bible offers is that God's will invites participation, not performance. Believers are not performing to earn approval. They are participating in what God is already doing. Paul expresses this beautifully: *"For we are co-workers in God's service."* (1 Corinthians 3:9). This partnership assumes imperfection. God does not wait for flawless execution before involving His people. He works through weakness, limitation, and growth.

Understanding God's will this way removes the crushing weight of needing to prove faithfulness through results. Believers contribute what they can, where they are, trusting that God integrates their faithfulness into His larger purposes.

Hope anchored beyond success and failure

The Bible consistently anchors hope beyond the ups and downs of visible life. Faithfulness is sustained not by immediate reward, but by confidence in God's future.

Paul expresses this hope clearly in 2 Corinthians 4:17, *"For our present troubles are achieving for us an eternal glory that far outweighs them all."* Hope lifts faith beyond temporary outcomes. God's will includes a future where faithfulness is fully revealed and restored. This eternal perspective does not diminish present responsibility. It strengthens it.

Paul says in 1 Corinthians 15:58, believers live faithfully now because they trust that nothing done in obedience is wasted. *"Your labour in the Lord is not in vain."*

Resting in God's evaluation

Perhaps the greatest freedom the Bible offers is release from self-evaluation. Believers are not called to constantly assess whether they have succeeded or failed in God's will. That judgment belongs to God. Paul states this plainly: *"It is the Lord who judges me."* (1 Corinthians 4:4). God's evaluation is gracious, just, and informed by perfect knowledge.

Believers are free to live honestly, repent when needed, and continue forward without the burden of self-condemnation. This does not remove accountability. It relocates it. Faithfulness is lived before God, not before internal scorecards or external approval.

A life secure in God's faithful purpose

As this chapter draws together, the central truth becomes unmistakable. God's will is not fragile. It does not rise and fall with success or failure. It is carried forward by God's faithfulness and expressed through lives that remain trusting, obedient, and hopeful.

The Bible clearly affirms this assurance with quiet strength: *"The Lord will fulfil his purpose for me; your love, Lord, endures forever."* (Psalm 138:8).

God completes what He begins. Believers are not left to secure His will through performance. They are invited to live within it through faith.

In this light, success and failure lose their power to define identity. Faithfulness takes their place.

Believers are able to rest in the confidence that as they trust God, act responsibly, and persevere in obedience, God's will is being faithfully worked out in their lives, not through flawless achievement, but through enduring relationship with the God who is faithful in every season.

16. RESTING IN GOD'S WILL: ASSURANCE, CONFIDENCE, AND PEACE

After exploring discernment, freedom, suffering, success, and failure, we now turn toward rest. Many believers carry an unspoken weariness when it comes to God's will. Even after gaining clarity, the habit of striving lingers. The Bible does not leave believers in that place. It consistently invites them into assurance, confidence, and peace rooted not in certainty about the future, but in trust in God's faithful care.

I want to now explore what it means to *rest* in God's will. Not to disengage from responsibility, but to live without anxiety, self-doubt, or fear of missing out on God's purposes.

Assurance rooted in God's initiative

Assurance begins with God, not with human performance. The Bible repeatedly grounds confidence in what God has done and continues to do, rather than in a believer's ability to discern perfectly. Paul expresses this assurance very clearly: *"Those God foreknew he also predestined to be conformed to the image of his Son."* (Romans 8:29).

God's will is anchored in His initiative. Long before believers begin to ask questions about guidance, God is already at work shaping them according to His purpose.

This assurance is reinforced throughout the Bible. *"The Lord will fulfil his purpose for me."* (Psalm 138:8). God does not begin a work only to abandon it. His will is not provisional or fragile. It is steady, intentional, and sustained by His faithfulness.

For believers, this means assurance does not depend on constant clarity or flawless obedience. It rests in the confidence that God remains committed to His people, even when they feel uncertain, tired, or overwhelmed.

God's will is not something believers must constantly secure. It is something God faithfully carries forward.

Confidence without control

Resting in God's will requires relinquishing the illusion of control. The Bible never promises us control over outcomes. It promises confidence grounded in trust.

Proverbs offers this steady counsel: *"Trust in the Lord with all your heart and lean not on your own understanding."* (Proverbs 3:5). Trust does not eliminate planning or responsibility. It removes the need to control results. Believers act wisely, but they do not carry the burden of guaranteeing success.

Jesus addresses this directly when He warns against anxious preoccupation with the future: *"Do not worry about tomorrow, for tomorrow will worry about itself."* (Matthew 6:34). Worry arises when responsibility becomes control. Confidence grows when responsibility is exercised within trust. This shift is subtle but vital. Believers remain active, thoughtful, and engaged. What changes is the posture of the heart. They are no longer driven by fear of getting it wrong. They trust that God is at work beyond what they can manage or foresee.

Peace that guards the heart

The Bible consistently presents peace as the fruit of trust, not the product of certainty. Peace does not require answers to every question. It flows from confidence in God's care.

Paul describes this peace with striking clarity: *"And the peace of God, which transcends all understanding, will guard your hearts and your minds in Christ Jesus."* (Philippians 4:7). This peace is not logical or explainable. It exists precisely when understanding is limited. Peace guards the heart against two common threats: anxiety and self-condemnation. When believers rest in God's will, they are freed from constant self-evaluation. They are no longer measuring each decision against imagined standards of perfection. They trust that God's grace covers their faithfulness.

This peace does not numb responsibility. It steadies it. Believers continue to make decisions, face challenges, and respond to change, but they do so without the inner turmoil that comes from fear of missing God's will.

Rest as an act of faith

Resting in God's will is not passivity. It is an act of faith. The Bible consistently treats rest as trust expressed bodily and spiritually. The writer to the Hebrews speaks of this rest explicitly: *"There remains, then, a Sabbath-rest for the people of God."* (Hebrews 4:9). This rest is not merely physical. It is a deep confidence that God's work does not depend entirely on human effort.

Jesus' invitation captures this beautifully when He said in Matthew 11:28, *"Come to me, all you who are weary and burdened, and I will give you rest."* The burden Jesus addresses is not responsibility itself, but the weight of striving to secure righteousness, approval, or certainty. Rest comes from trusting Him.

As believers learn to rest in God's will, something profound happens. The Christian life becomes lighter without becoming shallow. Responsibility remains, but anxiety loosens its grip. Faith becomes less about vigilance and more about trust.

This rest does not remove questions. It changes how believers live with them. God's will becomes not a source of pressure, but a place of refuge. And in that refuge, assurance, confidence, and peace begin to take root, preparing believers to live faithfully without fear as they continue walking with the God who is both sovereign and good.

If resting in God's will begins with assurance and grows into confidence, it is sustained through daily trust. The Bible does not present rest as a one-time achievement, but as a posture that must be returned to again and again. Believers learn to rest not by escaping responsibility, but by carrying it differently.

Learning to trust God with the weight of life

One of the reasons rest often feels elusive is that believers will carry weight that God never intended them to bear. They assume responsibility not only for obedience, but for outcomes, timing, and results. The Bible gently but firmly corrects this tendency.

Peter urges believers, *"Cast all your anxiety on him because he cares for you."* (1 Peter 5:7). The command to cast anxiety assumes that believers are carrying it. Rest begins when burdens are transferred back to God. This does not mean abandoning effort. It means relinquishing the illusion that everything depends on getting things right.

Jesus illustrates this difference when He contrasts heavy burdens with His own invitation: *"For my yoke is easy and my burden is light."* (Matthew 11:30). A yoke still implies work. What changes is who bears the weight. Rest comes from sharing responsibility with Christ rather than shouldering it alone. This trust is often learned slowly. Believers discover, sometimes through exhaustion, that striving does not produce peace. Trust does.

Peace that coexists with uncertainty

The Bible never promises a future free from uncertainty. It promises peace that exists within it. This distinction is crucial for resting in God's will. *"You will keep in perfect peace those whose minds are steadfast, because they trust in you."* (Isaiah 26:3). Peace here is not the result of resolved questions. It is the fruit of steadfast trust. Believers learn to live with unanswered questions without allowing them to dominate the heart.

This peace guards against constant mental replay. Instead of rehearsing decisions endlessly, believers entrust them to God. *"Commit to the Lord whatever you do, and he will establish your plans."* (Proverbs 16:3). Commitment does not require certainty. It requires trust expressed through action. Resting in God's will means accepting that clarity often comes later, if at all. Peace does not wait for understanding. It flows from confidence in God's care.

Freedom from self-condemnation

Another barrier to rest is self-condemnation. Believers may replay past decisions, wondering whether different choices would have produced better outcomes. The Bible offers a clear and liberating answer to this spiral. In Romans 8:1, Paul states it plainly: *"Therefore, there is now no condemnation for those who are in Christ Jesus."*

This declaration applies not only to moral failure, but to the fear of having failed God's will. God does not hold believers hostage to their past decisions. The Bible encourages believers to learn without being imprisoned by regret. *"Forget what is behind and strain toward what is ahead"* (Philippians 3:13). Forgetting does not mean denying responsibility. It means refusing to live under judgment that God Himself has removed.

Rest grows where grace is believed. When believers trust that God's acceptance is secure, they are freed to live forward rather than backward. God's will is not something they must defend by re-litigating the past. It is something they live into with hope.

Trust expressed through daily faithfulness

Resting in God's will does not produce passivity. It produces steady faithfulness. The Bible consistently links peace with obedience that is calm rather than frantic.

Paul exhorts believers, *"Let us not become weary in doing good."* (Galatians 6:9). Weariness often comes not from obedience itself, but from the pressure to control results. When believers rest in God's will, faithfulness becomes sustainable.

Daily faithfulness looks ordinary. It involves prayer, work, love, service, and perseverance. It does not require dramatic decisions or constant evaluation. The Bible honours this quiet consistency. *"Whatever you do, work at it with all your heart, as working for the Lord."* (Colossians 3:23).

As believers practise this kind of trust-filled obedience, rest deepens. God's will becomes less of a burden and more of a shelter. Responsibility remains real, but it is no longer heavy with fear.

In this way, rest becomes a lived reality rather than a distant ideal. Believers learn to trust God with the weight of life, to live peacefully amid uncertainty, to release self-condemnation, and to walk faithfully day by day. God's will is not something they must chase anxiously. It is the secure ground beneath their feet as they walk with the God who is faithful, present, and good.

As this chapter reaches its final movement, the invitation to rest becomes clearer and more settled. Resting in God's will is not a technique to master, but a way of living that flows from deep trust in God's character. It is the fruit of believing that God is both sovereign and good, and that His purposes are secure even when life remains complex.

Rest that flows from God's faithfulness

True rest is grounded not in a believer's ability to trust perfectly, but in God's unwavering faithfulness. The Bible consistently anchors assurance in who God is, not in how consistently His people respond.

Paul expresses this confidence plainly: *"If we are faithless, he remains faithful, for he cannot disown himself."* (2 Timothy 2:13). This does not excuse unfaithfulness, but it reassures weary believers that God's purposes do not collapse under human weakness. Rest grows as believers realise that God's will is sustained by His character, not by their vigilance.

This faithfulness of God is the reason rest is possible at all. Believers are not required to keep God's will on track. God is already doing that. They are invited to participate, not to manage.

Confidence that does not depend on certainty

Resting in God's will also reshapes the believer's relationship with certainty. The Bible never presents certainty as a prerequisite for peace. It presents trust as sufficient.

The psalmist captures this quiet confidence when he writes, *"I have calmed and quieted myself, I am like a weaned child with its mother."* (Psalm 131:2). The image is striking. The child is not anxious for answers. It rests in relationship. This is the posture the Bible invites believers to adopt toward God.

Confidence of this kind allows believers to live well even when questions remain. They make decisions, accept responsibility, and face uncertainty without panic. God's will is not threatened by what is unknown. It is upheld by God's presence within it.

Peace that shapes the whole life

When rest becomes a settled posture, peace begins to shape the whole of life. The Bible consistently describes peace as something that governs, guards, and directs the heart.

Paul urges us as believers, *"Let the peace of Christ rule in your hearts."* (Colossians 3:15). Peace here is not an emotion that comes and goes. It is a governing reality. It influences how believers think, decide, and respond. This peace does not eliminate difficulty. It steadies believers within it. They are no longer driven by fear of missing God's will or by anxiety over outcomes. They trust that God is present, faithful, and at work, even when circumstances remain unresolved.

A life lived from rest, not toward it

Perhaps the most important shift the Bible calls believers to make is this: rest is not the reward at the end of faithful living. It is the starting place. Believers live *from* rest, not *toward* it.

The writer to the Hebrews speaks of this rest as something believers enter by faith (Hebrews 4:3). It is not postponed until everything is clear or resolved. It is entered now through trust in Christ. From that place of rest, obedience becomes lighter, discernment calmer, and faith more resilient.

Jesus' invitation remains the final word: *"Come to me, all you who are weary and burdened, and I will give you rest."* (Matthew 11:28). This rest is not escape from responsibility. It is freedom from fear.

As believers learn to rest in God's will, the Christian life takes on a new steadiness. Questions may remain. Decisions will still be made. Suffering, change, success, and failure will still come. But beneath it all, there is rest.

God's will is no longer something to chase or fear. It is the gracious and faithful context in which believers live, move, and grow. Resting in that truth does not make life smaller. It makes it lighter, freer, and more deeply rooted in the God who is faithful in every season.

17. LIVING CONFIDENTLY IN GOD'S WILL

As this book reaches its final chapter, the focus shifts from explanation to embodiment. The question is no longer *What is God's will?* but *How do I live confidently within it?* The Bible does not invite believers to spend their lives analysing God's will from a distance. It calls them to live it, trust it, and walk forward with confidence grounded in God's faithfulness. I want to now draw together the central themes of this book and frame them pastorally. God's will is not something believers graduate into once they understand it fully. It is the reality in which they already live as people united with Christ.

Confidence rooted in union with Christ

The deepest source of confidence for the Christian is not discernment skill, maturity, or experience, but union with Christ. The Bible consistently places assurance here. Believers are not trying to stay close to God through correct decisions. They are already secure in Christ.

Paul expresses this assurance clearly: *"For you died, and your life is now hidden with Christ in God."* (Colossians 3:3). God's will for believers is inseparable from this union. Their lives are not exposed, fragile, or easily derailed. They are held securely in Christ. This truth radically reshapes confidence. Believers do not approach life as those who might step outside God's will at any moment. They live as those who belong to God, are known by Him, and are being shaped continually by His grace.

Union with Christ also means that God's will is personal, relational, and present. It is not an abstract plan hovering over life. It is the lived reality of Christ dwelling in believers and shaping them from within. *"Christ in you, the hope of glory."* (Colossians 1:27).

God's will as a way of life, not a target

Throughout the Bible, God's will is described in the language of walking, abiding, and living. It is not framed as a single moment of discovery, but as an ongoing way of life.

Paul urges believers, *"So then, just as you received Christ Jesus as Lord, continue to live your lives in him."* (Colossians 2:6). Receiving Christ and living in Him are part of the same movement. God's will does not begin after conversion. It is the context in which the Christian life unfolds from the beginning. This understanding dismantles the pressure to "get it right" at every turn. Believers are not aiming at a narrow target that can be missed with one wrong step. They are walking a path shaped by grace, truth, and trust. When missteps occur, they can be corrected within relationship, not punished from a distance.

The Bible affirms this steady guidance: *"The Lord makes firm the steps of the one who delights in him."* (Psalm 37:23). Steps are taken one at a time. God's will is lived progressively, not grasped all at once.

Living with courage rather than caution

A confident life within God's will is marked more by courage than caution. The Bible does not commend hesitation driven by fear. It consistently calls believers to boldness rooted in trust.

Paul encourages believers, *"Be strong in the Lord and in his mighty power."* (Ephesians 6:10). Strength here is not self-confidence. It is confidence drawn from God's presence and promises. Believers are invited to act, speak, and live faithfully without being paralysed by uncertainty. This courage does not eliminate humility. It coexists with dependence. Believers act decisively while remaining teachable. They plan wisely while holding outcomes loosely. They live responsibly without fear of missing God's will.

The book of Proverbs captures this balance: *"The righteous are as bold as a lion"* (Proverbs 28:1). Righteous boldness flows not from certainty about outcomes, but from confidence in God's faithfulness.

Confidence that grows through practice

The Bible assumes that confidence in God's will grows through lived faith. It is not downloaded instantly. It is cultivated through obedience, reflection, and trust over time.

The writer to the Hebrews describes mature believers as those *"who by constant use have trained themselves to distinguish good from evil."* (Hebrews 5:14). Confidence deepens as believers practise faithfulness in real situations. God's will becomes less abstract and more instinctive as trust matures.

This practice-oriented faith frees believers from waiting until they feel ready. Confidence often follows obedience rather than preceding it. As believers step forward in trust, they discover that God is already at work, guiding, sustaining, and shaping them along the way.

A secure place to stand

As this final chapter unfolds, one truth becomes increasingly clear: God's will is not a precarious place to stand. It is secure, gracious, and expansive. Believers are not balancing on the edge of error. They are standing on the solid ground of God's faithfulness.

Paul expresses this assurance beautifully: *"Therefore, my dear brothers and sisters, stand firm."* (1 Corinthians 15:58). Standing firm does not require perfect understanding. It requires trust in the God who is faithful.

Living confidently in God's will means embracing this security. It means walking forward with courage, responsibility, and peace, trusting that God is at work not only ahead, but beneath and around every step.

As this chapter continues, that confidence will be grounded even more deeply in the daily realities of Christian life, showing how believers can live with freedom, joy, and assurance, not because every question has been answered, but because the God who calls them is faithful and good.

If confidence is rooted in union with Christ and expressed through courage rather than caution, it must also find expression in everyday life. The Bible never confines confidence in God's will to moments of decision or spiritual intensity. It is meant to shape how believers live, relate, work, and serve day by day.

Confidence expressed in day-to-day faithfulness

One of the clearest biblical marks of confidence in God's will is faithfulness in ordinary life. The Bible repeatedly affirms that God's purposes are worked out not only through dramatic acts, but through steady obedience in everyday contexts.

Paul exhorts believers, *"Whatever you do, work at it with all your heart, as working for the Lord"* (Colossians 3:23). This instruction assumes confidence. Believers are not constantly questioning whether their daily tasks fall within God's will. They live as though all of life belongs to Him.

This ordinary faithfulness reflects trust. It says, *God is present here.* Confidence does not require a sense of calling for every action. It rests in the assurance that God is honoured when believers live responsibly, lovingly, and honestly wherever they are.

Such confidence removes the pressure to seek significance through constant change or heightened spiritual experiences. God's will is lived out in the rhythms of work, family, service, and rest.

Freedom from the need for constant reassurance

Another sign of growing confidence is freedom from the need for continual reassurance. Anxious faith seeks repeated confirmation. Confident faith rests in what God has already made clear.

The Bible consistently points believers back to God's revealed truth rather than encouraging endless searching. *"We live by faith, not by sight."* (2 Corinthians 5:7). Faith here is not blind optimism. It is settled trust in God's character and promises.

This does not mean believers stop praying or reflecting. It means prayer becomes relational rather than interrogative. Believers pray not to extract certainty, but to remain attentive and dependent. Confidence allows prayer to deepen rather than intensify. Freedom from constant reassurance also guards against over-spiritualising decisions.

Believers learn to distinguish between matters of obedience, which the Bible addresses clearly, and matters of wisdom, which require thought, counsel, and responsibility. Confidence allows both to coexist without anxiety.

Confidence that makes space for learning and growth

Living confidently in God's will does not imply that believers stop learning or growing. On the contrary, confidence creates space for growth by removing fear of failure.

The Bible encourages this posture of teachability. *"The righteous fall seven times, they rise again."* (Proverbs 24:16). Falling is not the defining feature. Rising is. Confidence in God's will allows believers to acknowledge mistakes without despair and to learn without self-condemnation.

Paul reflects this learning posture when he writes, *"Not that I have already obtained all this... but I press on."* (Philippians 3:12). Even maturity does not eliminate growth. It deepens humility and perseverance. Confidence rooted in God's faithfulness frees believers to take responsibility very seriously while remaining flexible and teachable. God's will is not threatened by growth. It is expressed through it.

A life marked by gratitude and joy

The Bible consistently links confidence in God's will with gratitude and joy. Anxiety drains joy. Trust restores it. Paul exhorts believers, *"Give thanks in all circumstances; for this is God's will for you in Christ Jesus."* (1 Thessalonians 5:18). Gratitude is not dependent on circumstances being ideal. It flows from confidence that God is present and faithful within them.

Joy functions similarly. It is not the result of everything going well, but the fruit of trust. *"The joy of the Lord is your strength"* (Nehemiah 8:10). Strength here is not emotional exuberance, but resilience rooted in assurance. A confident life before God is therefore not grim or burdened. It is marked by steadiness, gratitude, and joy that persist through change and uncertainty. God's will is not something to endure. It is something to live within, with freedom and hope.

Confidence that looks beyond self

Finally, confidence in God's will turns believers outward rather than inward. Anxiety produces introspection. Confidence will produce generosity.

Paul urges believers, *"Let us consider how we may spur one another on toward love and good deeds"* (Hebrews 10:24). When believers are no longer consumed with evaluating their own standing, they are freed to invest in others. God's will becomes outward-facing, expressed through love, service, and encouragement. This outward orientation reflects Christ Himself. Confidence in God's will is ultimately Christlike confidence: secure in the Father's love and free to give oneself for others.

As believers grow in this kind of confidence, the question of God's will no longer dominates their thoughts. It quietly shapes their lives. They live faithfully, gratefully, and generously, trusting that God is at work in and through them, not because they have mastered discernment, but because they belong to a faithful and gracious God.

As this study comes to an end, the question of God's will is finally laid to rest, not because every mystery has been solved, but because a deeper confidence has taken hold. The Bible does not call believers to certainty about the future. It calls them to trust in a faithful God and to live boldly within the freedom He has given.

A life no longer ruled by the question

For many believers, the question *"Am I in God's will?"* has functioned like a quiet anxiety humming beneath the surface of life. The Bible invites believers to release that anxiety. God's will is not something to be constantly checked or verified. It is the secure context of life in Christ.

Paul expresses this settled confidence simply: *"For we live by faith, not by sight."* (2 Corinthians 5:7). Faith here is not constant self-examination. It is trust expressed through obedience. Believers live forward, not backward, trusting that God is faithful to guide them as they walk.

This does not remove discernment. It relocates it. Discernment becomes a quiet attentiveness rather than a being consuming preoccupation. God's will becomes something believers live, not something they anxiously measure.

Confidence that holds freedom and responsibility together

At the heart of this book has been the conviction that God's will holds freedom and responsibility together in Christ. The Bible does not pit these against each other. It unites them.

Paul's words capture this balance perfectly: *"Work out your salvation with fear and trembling, for it is God who works in you to will and to act according to his good purpose."* (Philippians 2:12–13).

Responsibility and grace always operate together. Believers act faithfully because God is already at work within them. This balance guards against both passivity and pressure.

Believers are neither spectators nor controllers in life. They are participants in God's ongoing work, living responsibly within the freedom God provides.

Living well within God's will

To live confidently in God's will is not to live without questions, but to live without fear. It is to trust God's character more than one's own ability to discern.

The Bible consistently calls believers to this kind of life. *"Do not be anxious about anything."* (Philippians 4:6). This is not denial of responsibility. It is invitation to trust. As believers entrust their lives to God, peace becomes a steady companion rather than an occasional visitor.

Living well within God's will means embracing the ordinary and the uncertain with equal trust. It means making decisions wisely, loving generously, serving faithfully, and resting confidently in God's care. If this book leaves the reader with one conviction, let it be this: God is faithful. His will is not fragile. It does not depend on perfect discernment or flawless obedience. It rests on His unchanging character and gracious purposes.

The Bible affirms this again and again: *"The one who calls you is faithful, and he will do it."* (1 Thessalonians 5:24). God completes what He begins. Believers are not left to secure God's will by their own vigilance. They are invited to trust Him.

This faithfulness frees believers to live with courage, joy, and peace. They no longer need to fear missing God's will. They are already living within it as people united with Christ, guided by the Bible, shaped by wisdom, and sustained by grace.

A life lived forward in trust

As this book concludes, the invitation is simple and profound. Live forward. Trust God. Walk faithfully. Love deeply. Rest confidently.

God's will is not a puzzle to solve. It is the gracious purpose of a faithful God who calls His people to live fully and freely in Christ.

As believers embrace that truth, they discover that God's will is not something hidden or elusive. It is the steady, life-giving reality in which they already live.

And in that confidence, they are free.

www.ingramcontent.com/pod-product-compliance
Lightning Source LLC
Chambersburg PA
CBHW051729020426
42333CB00014B/1232